*The*

# HOW-TO
# COOKBOOK
*for* **TEENS**

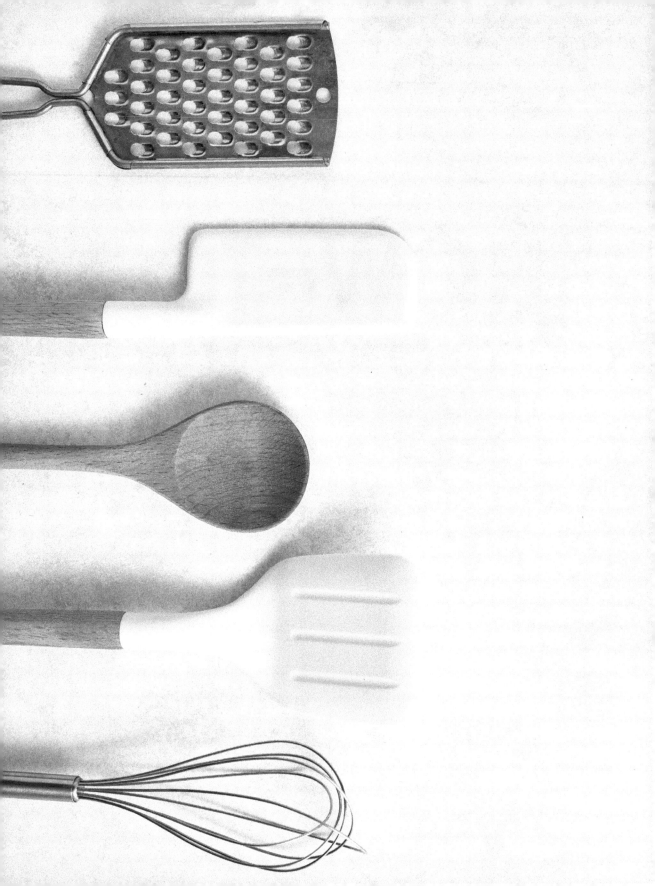

# The
# HOW-TO
# COOKBOOK
## for TEENS

## 100 Easy Recipes to Learn the Basics

### Julee Morrison

#### Photography by Jennifer Chong

ROCKRIDGE
PRESS

Interior and Cover Designer: Suzanne LaGasa
Photo Art Director/Art Manager: Michael Hargrove
Editor: Marjorie DeWitt
Production Editor: Ashley Polikoff
Photography © 2019 Jennifer Chong. Food styling by Elizabeth Normoyle.

ISBN: Print 978-1-64611-419-1 | eBook 978-1-64611-420-7

R0

For Jake, Zac, Kyra, Abi, MacKenzie, and William

# CONTENTS

Chapter 8:

# DESERTS, 135

# INTRODUCTION

**WELCOME!** I'm excited you're here and want to learn how to be a teen chef. Cooking is such a great skill, and it's fun! This book is going to teach you how to feed yourself, not just now, but long-term. It's going to fire up your curiosity to try new foods, broaden your palate, and teach you how plain food can be deliciously transformed by a recipe.

We'll cover the rules of cooking, but we'll also have fun, get messy (and learn how to clean up afterward), and, most important, create amazing food and memories.

The recipes in this book start with the fundamentals, like how to make eggs. The basic recipes will help you learn a technique or skill and develop confidence. Once you have a good foundation, learning to cook is nothing more than the process of layering your skills to make more complex recipes. For example, I will teach you to make eggs scrambled, fried, and boiled, then I'll help you elevate those skills by making eggs in a basket, deviled eggs, breakfast muffins, and omelets.

In addition to helping you develop and layer your cooking skills, I will teach you organizational skills, safety measures, and some great hacks. You'll find information on how to set up your stations, how to accurately measure wet and dry ingredients, how to safely use a knife, and how to avoid burns. I'll share with you my hack for icing a cake perfectly in a matter of minutes (page 141) and how to make Easy Crispy Oven Bacon (page 28) without the mess and worry of grease splatter.

I encourage you to practice. You will have great successes, but you'll also have some fails. That's okay. Don't get discouraged. It happens. The important thing is that you keep cooking and learn from what went wrong.

Listen to feedback. I always make a recipe just as the recipe says the first time. Then, I listen to what the people eating it say, and I write their comments on a sticky note and stick it on the recipe for reference the next time I make it.

Be an adventurous eater. Savor each bite and learn about the flavors that you taste, how they complement one another and the texture of the food. Think about what ingredients make up the dish and take a moment to observe how it is plated.

I love to test new recipes and try new foods. Cooking can be a creative outlet, and the reward is a delicious meal and a satisfying feeling of accomplishment. What I like best about cooking, though, is that it's a great way to bring family and friends together.

I hope you make everything in this book and fill the book with your notes to make the recipes your own. I hope you share your creations with your friends and with your family. But most of all, I hope you have fun.

Let's get started!

# Chapter 1

# HOW TO PREPARE LIKE A CHEF

I'm so excited you're on this journey to learn to cook like a pro. I want you to be successful, and the first thing I want to teach you is how to prepare like a chef.

There is a French culinary phrase, *mise en place*, which means "everything in its place." It's a great philosophy to practice as a chef. Think of it as every mixing bowl, every spice, and every tool having its own designated place in the kitchen so you can work smoothly and efficiently.

This chapter will walk you through getting oriented and organized in the kitchen so you can be successful.

# Essential Tools

Cooking is easier and faster with the right equipment. Look around your kitchen. Some—or all—of the items that you'll need may already be in your drawers and cupboards, including:

Knives. A chef's knife is the primary knife you will use in the kitchen. It is about 8 inches long and 1½ inches wide. It can be used to slice, chop, dice, and mince. Also consider a paring knife (a small knife for peeling and coring fruits and vegetables) and a serrated knife (a scallop-edged knife for cutting breads).

> CAUTION! *Nothing is worse than a dull knife! Contrary to popular belief, a dull knife is more dangerous than a sharp one. A dull blade rips and tears because it requires more pressure in order to do the job. The added pressure also increases the chance of slippage. For safety and efficiency, use sharp knives.*

Cutting boards. You'll need two separate cutting boards, one for meat, poultry, and seafood, and another for everything else. Wood, bamboo, or plastic cutting boards are best for your knives.

Measuring cups. Look for a set of measuring cups that includes the ¼ cup, ⅓ cup, ½ cup, and 1 cup sizes for dry ingredients and a large glass measuring cup for liquids.

Measuring spoons. Measuring spoons are used to measure smaller amounts of dry or liquid ingredients. The ideal set will contain measuring spoons for ⅛ teaspoon, ¼ teaspoon, ½ teaspoon, 1 teaspoon, and 1 tablespoon.

Mixing bowls. Mixing bowls are your go-to for mixing together marinades, sauces, batters, and more. A set of three—one small, one medium, and one large—will get you started.

Colander. A colander is a great tool for draining pasta, washing vegetables, and draining canned ingredients.

Whisk. One of the most used items in my kitchen, a whisk can be used to make salad dressings and sauces, beat eggs, and combine wet or dry ingredients.

Box grater. The grater is a multipurpose tool. It serves as a grater and a zester.

Skillet. You'll need a skillet for sautéing and frying. A 10-inch skillet will get you started.

Saucepan. Saucepans are for cooking soups, pastas, and sauces. A small (1½ quart) and medium saucepan (4 quart) are good starters.

Large pot. A 6-quart pot is ideal for the larger soup, stew, and pasta recipes.

Baking sheet. Indispensable for baking cookies, baking sheets are also great for roasting vegetables or making nachos for a crowd. Look for a jelly roll pan, or a baking sheet with a lip, which is more versatile and prevents overflow.

Muffin pan. Choose one with either 6 or 12 built-in muffin cups.

Baking pan. This is a large, deep dish with high edges that is oven-proof. The most common sizes and shapes are an 8-by-8-inch square or a 9-by-13-inch rectangle.

Rubber spatula. This is a wide flexible cooking tool used for scraping wet ingredients out of a bowl or pan, as well as mixing and folding.

Turner spatula. This is a tool with a hard, wide, flat end used for flipping eggs, pancakes, French toast, hamburgers, etc.

Cooking spoons. Look for a small assortment of cooking spoons, including a wooden spoon, stirring spoon, slotted spoon, and ladle, which are all very helpful in the kitchen.

Tongs. These are used to grip and lift objects instead of holding them directly with your hands.

Oven mitts. These protect your hands and forearms when taking hot items out of the oven.

Digital cooking thermometer. This will help ensure food is cooked to the proper temperature.

Blender. A traditional blender or an immersion blender will help you make smoothies, sauces, and soups.

# Microwave Hacks

Microwaves do so much more than just heating leftovers. I remember when my family got our first microwave and my mother cooked our entire Thanksgiving dinner, including the turkey, in the microwave.

Cooking things like bacon, baked potatoes, and dried beans are known for being easier and quicker in the microwave. But did you know that zapping a lemon for 20 seconds makes it easier to juice? Or that you can microwave cake frosting for about 30 seconds (or until a uniformly thin consistency) and pour it over a cake for a perfectly smooth frosting?

You can even use the microwave for cleanup. Sanitize your scrubby kitchen sponges by saturating them with water and microwaving for 1 minute, or disinfect small wooden cutting boards by putting them in the microwave for 30 seconds to 1 minute.

# Safety First

Whether you're a novice cook or an experienced chef, kitchen safety is a priority, and safety starts with prevention. Review the following safety precautions before getting started in the kitchen.

## FIRES

To prevent kitchen fires, take the following precautions:

- Keep a fire extinguisher near the stove.
- Make sure the smoke alarms in your home are in working order.
- Familiarize yourself with what to do in case of a fire.
- Do not leave anything you are cooking on the stove unattended.
- Do not put metal of any kind (metal bowls, silverware, aluminum foil, etc.) into the microwave.

If a fire should break out, act quickly and respond appropriately:

- **Fire in a cooking pan on the stove.** Do NOT move the pan. Wearing an oven mitt, place a lid on the pan to smother the flames. Turn off the stove. If you cannot safely put the lid on the pan, use a fire extinguisher, targeting the base of the fire.
- **Grease fire.** Do NOT use water! Instead, throw baking soda or salt on the flames, or use a fire extinguisher.
- **Fire in the oven or microwave.** Leave the door closed to suffocate the flames. Turn the appliance off immediately.

If the fire is spreading and you can't control it, get everyone out of the house and call 911.

## BURNS

Burns occur when hot water, hot oil, steam, or hot metal come in contact with the skin. To prevent burns:

- Turn pan handles away from other burners and away from the edge of the stove.
- Wear an apron, tie your hair back, and do not wear long loose sleeves while cooking.
- Keep oven mitts near the stove.
- Never touch the stovetop or an oven rack with your bare hands.
- Stand back when cooking with hot water, hot oil, and other hot liquids.

## CUTS

Most cuts in the kitchen are caused by knives, so let's talk about knife safety:

- Always cut away from your body.
- Don't lick knives.
- Don't use a knife to pry open canned goods.
- Never drop a knife into a sink of dishwater. Instead, wash it immediately and put it away.

## BACTERIA

Bacteria are invisible but can cause mild to severe illness. To avoid bacterial infection, be sure to:

- Always wash your hands before you start cooking and frequently throughout the cooking process, and definitely after handling any raw meat, fish, or uncooked eggs.
- Keep raw meat, eggs, fish, and dairy refrigerated when not in use.
- Refrigerate anything with meat, fish, eggs, and dairy within two hours of cooking.
- Wash your cutting boards after each use.
- Cook meat to the recommended internal temperature.
- Do not put food on a plate that has had raw meat on it.
- Do not eat raw eggs or batters with raw eggs.

# 7 Tips for Being a Good Cook

Cooking doesn't have to be intimidating. It just takes a little knowledge and practice to be successful in the kitchen.

1. **Keep a kitchen towel within arm's reach.**
   You can use it to dry your hands after washing, place a cutting board on it to keep the cutting board stationary, and clean up spills when necessary.

2. **Do prep work before you start cooking.**
   Before you do anything else, take out the equipment you'll need. Then, measure, cut, peel, slice, and grate all of your ingredients so that you can move through your recipe smoothly.

3. **Measure your ingredients.**
   Spoon dry ingredients, such as flour and sugar, into a dry measuring cup and level off for accurate measuring. Use a glass measuring cup to measure liquids.

4. **Season to taste.**
   Salt and other seasonings are meant to elevate the flavors of food. Taste what you're making, then add the seasonings and taste again. If you think more seasoning is needed, only add a little at a time, then stir and taste after each addition, so you don't end up with overly salty or spicy food.

5. **Use a digital thermometer.**
   Especially when cooking meats, use a digital thermometer to check for doneness. Beef, pork, lamb, and seafood should be cooked to 145°F, ground meats to 160°F, and poultry to 165°F.

6. **Clean as you go.**
   This will make clean up easier after you're finished cooking.

7. **Be an adventurous eater.**
   Try new things when you can. As you're eating, think about the look, smell, taste, and texture of the food. If you don't like something, try it again, in a different form. I think okra is slimy, but I really like fried okra. There are a lot of chocolate cakes; find one you love, and explore what it is that sets it apart from the others. Never write off a food after one try!

# Chapter 2

# HOW TO COOK LIKE A CHEF

While practice will help you perfect your favorite dish, there are other things that will help you on your journey to cook like a chef.

In this chapter, we'll review cooking terminology and cover the basics of setting up your station, reading a recipe, measuring, mixing, and some basic knife skills. Each of these skills builds upon one another. They are all important to your success.

# Setting Up Your Station

Always start with a clean kitchen. A clean kitchen will help you prevent contamination and avoid kitchen accidents. Keep a dish towel near the sink so you can wash and dry your hands frequently. Keep a separate towel, or paper towels, close by to quickly address any spills and clean as you go.

Take out the equipment you will need. This will keep you from having to stop and look for things as you make your recipe. If you will be working with a cutting board, place a damp paper towel or nonstick pad underneath it. This will keep it from moving as you work. In this book, you will find tools and equipment lists included with each recipe. These will include some of the essential tools, but you should always take out your cutting board and a chef's knife. Chances are, you will need them, so it's always a good idea to have them on hand.

Gather all of your ingredients, prep them, and put them in a place that is easily accessible. If they need to stay refrigerated or frozen, just make sure they're in a place where you can get to them easily.

# Cooking Terminology

Cooking has its own language. You can reference this guide of cooking terminology when you're unsure about something in a recipe or even to test your knowledge.

**Beat:** To incorporate air and make a mixture smooth by mixing rapidly by hand or with an electric mixer.

**Blend:** To thoroughly combine multiple ingredients.

**Boil:** To cook in boiling liquid.

**Chop:** To cut into pieces with a knife.

**Cream:** To work butter or shortening (sometimes combined with sugar) with the back of a spoon or an electric mixer until light and fluffy.

**Dredge:** To lightly coat with flour or bread crumbs.

**Grease:** To coat the interior surface of a baking pan or dish with butter, or another fat, to prevent food from sticking to the pan as it cooks.

**Preheat:** To heat the oven to a specified temperature before putting in the food to cook.

**Simmer:** To cook in liquid just below the boiling point. Bubbles will break at the surface but at a much slower rate than at a full boil.

**Heat settings:** When you see "medium-low," "medium," and "medium-high" in a recipe, be aware that stoves vary and it's best to think of the heat as it would cook butter:

> **Low** = Butter in the pan will melt slowly, bubble gently, and take so long to brown that you'll get bored waiting for it.

> **Medium** = Butter will melt quickly, bubble vigorously, and brown quickly.

> **High** = Butter will melt at an alarming speed, bubble violently, and brown in a matter of seconds.

# How to Read a Recipe

Carefully reading a recipe will help you be successful. Before you start to cook, read the recipe all the way through. If you aren't familiar with a term, technique, method, or ingredient, look it up. Then read the recipe all the way through a second time to make sure you understand the steps.

After you read the recipe at least twice, take out your equipment and begin gathering, prepping, and measuring out your ingredients.

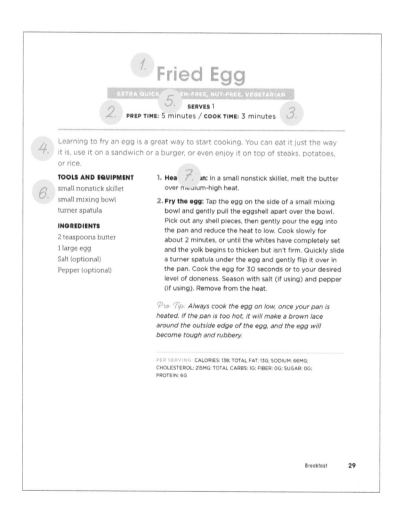

*1.* **Fried Egg**

EXTRA QUICK, ~~EN-FREE, NUT-FREE, VEGETARIAN~~

*5.* **SERVES** 1

*2.* **PREP TIME:** 5 minutes / **COOK TIME:** 3 minutes *3.*

*4.* Learning to fry an egg is a great way to start cooking. You can eat it just the way it is, use it on a sandwich or a burger, or even enjoy it on top of steaks, potatoes, or rice.

**TOOLS AND EQUIPMENT**

*6.* small nonstick skillet
small mixing bowl
turner spatula

**INGREDIENTS**

2 teaspoons butter
1 large egg
Salt (optional)
Pepper (optional)

1. **Hea** *7.* **an:** In a small nonstick skillet, melt the butter over medium-high heat.

2. **Fry the egg:** Tap the egg on the side of a small mixing bowl and gently pull the eggshell apart over the bowl. Pick out any shell pieces, then gently pour the egg into the pan and reduce the heat to low. Cook slowly for about 2 minutes, or until the whites have completely set and the yolk begins to thicken but isn't firm. Quickly slide a turner spatula under the egg and gently flip it over in the pan. Cook the egg for 30 seconds or to your desired level of doneness. Season with salt (if using) and pepper (if using). Remove from the heat.

*Pro Tip: Always cook the egg on low, once your pan is heated. If the pan is too hot, it will make a brown lace around the outside edge of the egg, and the egg will become tough and rubbery.*

PER SERVING: CALORIES: 138; TOTAL FAT: 13G; SODIUM: 66MG; CHOLESTEROL: 215MG; TOTAL CARBS: 1G; FIBER: 0G; SUGAR: 0G; PROTEIN: 6G

Breakfast    **29**

1. **Title**

2. **Prep time:** approximate time needed to prep the recipe

3. **Cook time:** approximate time needed to cook the recipe

4. **Headnote:** an introduction to the recipe

5. **Yield:** amount the recipe will make or how many it will serve

6. **Ingredient list:** the ingredients needed to make the recipe listed in the order they are used

7. **Directions:** step-by-step instructions for making the recipe

The first time you make a recipe, follow the directions exactly as given. Even a slight change in the process can lead to mediocre results. Once you've made a recipe successfully, you can experiment with the seasonings or ingredients that affect the flavor. However, when baking, you should never alter fat, flour, baking powder, or the amount of liquid.

# Measuring Skills

Measuring is the key to your success when cooking. Cooking is a science, and by using the measurements specified in the recipe, you will get consistent results.

## DRY INGREDIENTS

Dry ingredients are typically measured in measuring cups or measuring spoons. Always level off the top with the flat edge of a kitchen knife for the most accurate measure. A measuring cup with ingredients heaping, or not filled completely, will affect your recipe results.

When measuring flour, be aware that it packs as it sits. For the most accurate measure you should sift the flour into a measuring cup, then, without tapping, level it off. Never dip the measuring cup into the flour and never tap the cup as you fill it, or your measurement will be inaccurate.

## LIQUIDS

To measure liquids, ideally you want to use a clear cup with graduated lines of measurement and a spout for easy pouring. To get an accurate measure of liquids, place the measuring cup on a level surface, and fill the cup exactly to the level desired. Bend down so the lines are at eye level to read the measurement correctly.

For best results when using the same cups or measuring spoons for wet and dry ingredients, you'll want to measure the dry ingredients first, followed by oils, then liquids like water.

# Mixing Skills

Most recipes will have you mix wet and dry ingredients separately. It's a crucial step in your success. When you mix the dry ingredients by themselves, you evenly disperse the spices, sugar, and raising agents. This keeps one cookie from having all the salt.

By using the method of mixing wet ingredients separately from dry ingredients, you will have better results and a more even texture and consistent flavor in your finished product.

There are different words used to describe how to combine ingredients. You'll find the following terms used in the recipes in this book, as well as in other recipes.

## STIR

This means blending ingredients with a circular motion. When you stir, you are making a liquid smooth and creating a uniform flavor. When you stir something while it's on the stove, you are keeping the ingredients moving in the pan to promote even cooking and prevent burning.

You will encounter terms such as "stir occasionally," "stir continuously," or "stir frequently" in recipes.

Typically, you "stir continuously," or without any breaks, when you want to thicken a liquid with a starch or protein. Something with dairy is to be "stirred continuously" to keep the dairy from scorching.

You would "stir frequently," or with a few breaks, when you add solids to a liquid, or when you want to thicken the sauce by reduction. Gravy would be an example: You want the solid (flour or cornstarch) to react with the liquid to become thicker.

When you "stir occasionally," you stir just enough to keep the heat even and prevent the food from being burned.

## FOLD

This action usually applies to whipped cream or beaten egg whites. The object is to combine lighter ingredients, like whipped cream or egg whites, with heavier ingredients, such as batter, without losing the air beaten into the cream or eggs. You pass a spoon down through the mixture, then pass the spoon across the bottom, bringing up some of the mixture to the top. Repeat until combined.

## WHISK

When you whisk, you are beating ingredients (such as heavy whipping cream, eggs, salad dressings, or sauces) with a fork or whisk to mix, blend, or incorporate air.

## TOSS

When you "toss," you use a light lift and drop method. You turn the food over and mix together. If you are "tossing" a salad, you would lift up the lettuce and gently flip it over to coat all sides of the lettuce.

# Knife Skills

Holding a knife correctly is the key to safety. Learning to hold a knife will also help you make precise and consistent cuts and give your food a more professional appearance.

## HOW TO HOLD A KNIFE

**How to hold a knife**

A knife has two major parts: the blade and the handle. Where the handle meets the blade is called the bolster. The sharp part of the blade is called the edge.

When you grip the knife, be sure to keep your hand behind the bolster and well away from the edge. Use your dominant hand and curl your fingers around the handle of the knife. Your thumb should be over the knife handle. The knife handle should fit comfortably in your hand.

When cutting foods, make sure that both the cutting board and the food itself are stable.

# SLICE

To slice is to cut thin pieces or strips of vegetables, fruits, meats, or breads. Meats should be sliced across the grain to keep the meat tender. When cutting vegetables, keep them stable on the cutting board by cutting them in half or cutting off a small section and placing the flat surface against the cutting board. As you are slicing, keep the blade in constant contact with your cutting board.

To slice a tomato: Hold the tomato firmly with your non-knife hand. Using a paring knife, insert the tip ¼-inch near the core and rotate your knife around the stem (1). Put the knife down, and pull out the stem. Place the tomato, stem-side down, on the cutting board. Using your non-knife hand, curl your fingers under to hold the tomato in place and keep them away from the knife. Starting on one side and working across the tomato, use a chef's knife to cut ½-inch vertical slices (2).

**How to slice 1**

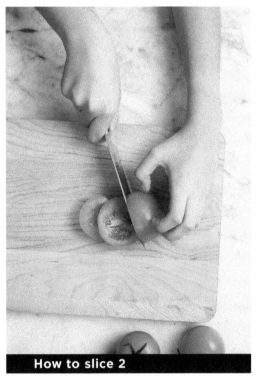

**How to slice 2**

# ROUGH CHOP

A rough chop is a way to cut larger chunks (about ½-inch to 1-inch square). A rough chop is larger and less exact than a dice or mince.

To chop an apple: Using a vegetable peeler, remove the skin, if desired. Slice off the bottom of the apple so it rests flat on the cutting board. Cut the apple in half lengthwise. Cut a "V" around the core lengthwise, and remove it. Lay the flat interior side of the apple against the cutting board. Using your non-knife hand, curl your fingers under to hold the apple and cut it into about ½-inch vertical slices (1). On the broad side, cut the slices in half lengthwise. They should now look like wide "sticks." Turn the "sticks" 90° and chop them into roughly ½-inch cubes (2).

How to chop 1

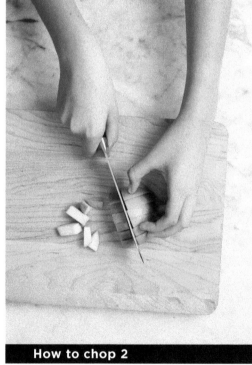

How to chop 2

# DICE

To dice is to cut the food into small, uniform cubes.

To dice an onion: Using a chef's knife, cut the top of the onion off and discard. Place the flat, cut-side down, on a cutting board, and cut the onion in half. Peel the onion. Then, place one of the halves, cut-side down again, on the cutting board. Stopping just short of the root end (leave it intact to keep the onion together), cut ¼-inch vertical slices (1). Turn the onion 90° and cut into the onion horizontally (your knife will be parallel to the cutting board) in ¼-inch increments. (Again, keep the root end intact.) Then, starting from the top and working your way to the root end, slice the onion crosswise in ¼-inch increments (2). As you do this, ¼-inch cubes will fall from the onion and accumulate at the cut end. Repeat with the other half.

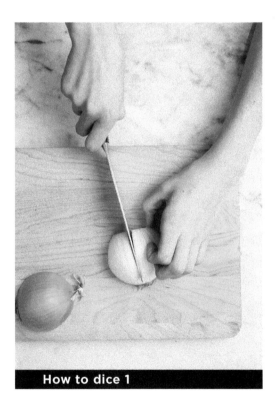

How to dice 1

How to dice 2

## MINCE

To mince means to cut into very small pieces (⅛-inch square or smaller).

To mince a clove of garlic: Cut off the root end. Put the garlic clove on the cutting board. Place the blade of a chef's knife flat against the clove with the edge facing away from you. With your palm flat against the knife blade and your fingers up, press down on the blade to gently crush the clove (1). Remove the papery skin. Roughly chop the garlic clove. Turn the blade to normal cutting position, and place your non-knife hand on top of the knife blade, keeping your fingers and thumb up. Rock the blade back and forth, up and down, cutting the garlic into fine pieces (2). Use the knife blade to scrape the garlic into a pile and repeat until the garlic is very small and almost a paste-like consistency.

How to mince 1

How to mince 2

# Other Cuts

One of the most versatile pieces of equipment in your kitchen is a box grater. It offers four sides that help you cut small pieces of food in a variety of ways.

### GRATE

To cut food into small strips using the large holes on a box grater. Common foods that you might grate include cheese, carrots, or zucchini. You might also grate apples for oatmeal using this side of the grater.

### SHRED

To tear or cut into thin pieces or strips. For meat, you can do this with two forks, two knives, or sometimes with an electric mixer. Shred cooked chicken breasts. For vegetables or cheeses, use the medium-size holes on a box grater.

### ZEST

To cut small shavings or particles, usually of the outer skin of citrus fruits. You can use a handheld zester or the smallest set of holes on a box grater.

### PEEL

To remove the outer covering of something like a banana, or other fruit or vegetables. This can be done by hand or with a tool depending on what you are peeling. Tools you can use include a paring knife, a vegetable peeler, or the smile-shaped slicing blades on the side of a box grater.

# Cooking in a Pan

These three cooking processes are closely related, are all relatively quick, and use medium-high to high heat, but the amount of oil or fat that you use varies.

## SAUTÉ

Sautéing is when you use a small amount of oil and high heat to quickly cook food. The fast cooking keeps the flavors sharp. Warm the pan over medium-high heat, add minimal fat, then add the food you are sautéing. Stir frequently.

## FRY

Frying is cooking food in hot oil. To fry, you will heat the oil in the pan over medium-high to high heat, then when it reaches the desired temperature, place the food in the oil to cook.

The difference between frying and sautéing is that sautéing uses direct heat, while frying is done by immersing the food in the hot oil.

## SEAR

Searing browns the surface of meats, quickly creating a crust that seals in moisture. It can be done in a skillet or on a grill. This method uses very little oil and is done at high heat for a short time.

# Cooking in an Oven

Methods of cooking in the oven are differentiated primarily by heat source and temperature.

## BAKE

To cook in the dry heat in an oven. It usually is done at lower temperatures—up to 375°F. Baking usually involves foods that start as a batter or dough.

## ROAST

To cook food in an uncovered pan in the dry heat of an oven at a temperature of at least 400°F. Roasting usually involves foods that have structure, like meats and vegetables.

## BROIL

To cook under the direct, top-down heat of a broiler. This method differs from baking and roasting, since the food is turned during the process and cooks only on one side at a time, rather than on all sides evenly.

# About the Recipes

You can make the recipes in this book all on your own with little effort. You'll find everything from breakfast recipes, like Fried Egg (page 29) and Oatmeal (page 32) to desserts like 3-Ingredient Peanut Butter Cookies (page 140) and Microwave Chocolate Mug Cake (page 145). Discover new snacks and sides, like Tortilla Chips (page 46) or Pull-Apart Pizza Bread (page 53). You'll find solo meals, like Vegetarian Burrito Bowl (page 99) and Steak and Eggs (page 38), for when you only need to feed yourself, or recipes to impress your family like Tater Tot Casserole (page 124) or Famous Chicken (page 116). This book will also show you how to make soups and salads like Vegetarian Chili (page 75) and Cobb Salad (page 88).

In addition, each recipe has a tip and a series of labels. The tips will give helpful hints, ideas for jazzing up a recipe, substitution suggestions, storage information, or special "pro-tips," which will have you cooking like a chef in no time. The labels will let you know if a recipe can be made quickly or if it is acceptable for people with dietary restrictions. Labels include:

- **Extra Quick.** The recipe can be completed start-to-finish in 30 minutes or less.
- **Nut-Free.** The recipe does not include nuts of any kind.
- **Gluten-Free.** The recipe does not include any ingredients that contain gluten. Always check ingredient packaging for gluten-free labeling in order to ensure foods, especially oats, were processed in a completely gluten-free facility.
- **Dairy-Free.** The recipe does not include any ingredients that contain dairy products.
- **Vegetarian.** The recipe does not contain any meat or fish but does contain dairy or eggs.
- **Vegan.** The recipe does not include meat, dairy, eggs, or any ingredients made with animal products.

All of the recipes in this book are for beginners and will teach you the basic cooking skills, techniques, methods, and fun hacks that will put you on the path to becoming a teen chef.

# Chapter 3

# BREAKFAST

I've heard it said that breakfast is the most important meal of the day. This chapter has you covered. You'll learn how to fry an egg (page 29), as well as make French Toast (page 33) and Easy Crispy Oven Bacon (page 28). There's breakfast for when you're pressed for time like an Omelet (page 31) or Oatmeal (page 32), and there are things to make ahead for those mornings when you're in grab-and-go mode, like Homemade Peanut Butter and Jelly Hand Pies (page 42) or Cheesy Breakfast Bacon Muffins (page 41).

The first meal of the day starts here.

# Easy Crispy Oven Bacon

**MAKES** 16 to 20 slices

**PREP TIME:** 5 minutes / **COOK TIME:** 15 minutes

Bacon is delicious, but making it can be messy and even a bit scary due to the grease splatter. I like making bacon in the oven. It's so easy, and there is no mess and no worry. It also allows you to cook an entire pound of bacon at one time and make it as crispy as you like it. This recipe is for regular bacon (1/16-inch-thick slices). If you want to use thick-cut bacon, increase the cooking time to 12 to 20 minutes.

**TOOLS AND EQUIPMENT**

baking sheet

tongs

oven mitts

**INGREDIENTS**

1 pound sliced bacon

1. **Prepare the bacon:** Preheat the oven to 400°F. Line a baking sheet with aluminum foil. Fold 2 paper towels in half. Place one on a plate and set the second paper towel aside. Lay the strips of bacon flat on the aluminum foil.

2. **Bake:** Place the baking sheet on the top rack of the oven, and bake for 8 to 15 minutes, or until the bacon has cooked to your desired level of crispiness. Carefully remove the baking sheet from the oven (there will be a layer of hot grease on the baking sheet, so keep it steady). Using tongs or a fork, transfer the bacon to the plate with the paper towel. Once your bacon covers the first paper towel, place the second paper towel over the bacon and stack the remaining bacon on top of the second paper towel. Let cool before serving.

*Store It: Make the bacon ahead of time, and store in a resealable sandwich bag so you have it for other recipes.*

PER SERVING (2 SLICES): CALORIES: 82; TOTAL FAT: 6G; SODIUM: 376MG; CHOLESTEROL: 18MG; TOTAL CARBS: 0G; FIBER: 0G; SUGAR: 0G; PROTEIN: 6G

# Fried Egg

EXTRA QUICK, GLUTEN-FREE, NUT-FREE, VEGETARIAN

**SERVES** 1

**PREP TIME:** 5 minutes / **COOK TIME:** 3 minutes

Learning to fry an egg is a great way to start cooking. You can eat it just the way it is, use it on a sandwich or a burger, or even enjoy it on top of steaks, potatoes, or rice.

## TOOLS AND EQUIPMENT

small nonstick skillet

small mixing bowl

turner spatula

## INGREDIENTS

2 teaspoons butter

1 large egg

Salt (optional)

Pepper (optional)

1. **Heat the pan:** In a small nonstick skillet, melt the butter over medium-high heat.

2. **Fry the egg:** Tap the egg on the side of a small mixing bowl and gently pull the eggshell apart over the bowl. Pick out any shell pieces, then gently pour the egg into the pan and reduce the heat to low. Cook slowly for about 2 minutes, or until the whites have completely set and the yolk begins to thicken but isn't firm. Quickly slide a turner spatula under the egg and gently flip it over in the pan. Cook the egg for 30 seconds or to your desired level of doneness. Season with salt (if using) and pepper (if using). Remove from the heat.

*Pro Tip: Always cook the egg on low, once your pan is heated. If the pan is too hot, it will make a brown lace around the outside edge of the egg, and the egg will become tough and rubbery.*

PER SERVING: CALORIES: 138; TOTAL FAT: 13G; SODIUM: 66MG; CHOLESTEROL: 215MG; TOTAL CARBS: 1G; FIBER: 0G; SUGAR: 0G; PROTEIN: 6G

# Egg in a Basket

**SERVES** 1

**PREP TIME:** 5 minutes / **COOK TIME:** 15 minutes

This is also known as Toad-in-a-Hole or Cookie-Cutter-Egg Toast. It's a one-pan breakfast where you cook the egg in a hole in a piece of bread—as the egg cooks, the bread also toasts.

## TOOLS AND EQUIPMENT

2-inch circular cookie cutter (or butter knife)

small nonstick skillet and lid

turner spatula

small mixing bowl

## INGREDIENTS

2 teaspoons butter

1 bread slice

1 large egg

1. **Prepare the bread:** Butter both sides of the bread. Using a 2-inch circular cookie cutter or butter knife, cut out a hole in the center of the bread slice. Preheat a small nonstick skillet by placing it over medium-low heat for 2 minutes before cooking. Put the bread in the skillet and cook for 5 minutes, or until golden. Using a turner spatula, turn the bread over.

2. **Cook the egg:** While the first side of the bread toasts, break the egg into a small mixing bowl, and remove any shells. After flipping the bread, slide the egg into the hole in the bread and cover the skillet with a lid. Cook slowly for about 5 minutes, or until the whites have set and the yolk begins to thicken but is not firm.

*Pro Tip:* *The larger you cut the hole, the less time your egg will need to cook, since it will spread out.*

PER SERVING: CALORIES: 208; TOTAL FAT: 14G; SODIUM: 178MG; CHOLESTEROL: 215MG; TOTAL CARBS: 13G; FIBER: 2G; SUGAR: 2G; PROTEIN: 10G

# Omelet

**SERVES** 1
**PREP TIME:** 5 minutes / **COOK TIME:** 5 minutes

An omelet is made by beating eggs and then cooking them until set. It is then folded in half, often around a filling. Omelets are a versatile meal. They can be plain with just the eggs, or you can add fillings and personalize them with your favorite flavors.

## TOOLS AND EQUIPMENT

small nonstick skillet

small mixing bowl

fork

rubber spatula

turner spatula

## INGREDIENTS

2 large eggs

2 tablespoons water

⅛ teaspoon salt

1 tablespoon butter

3 tablespoons shredded Cheddar cheese

1. **Heat the pan:** Heat a small nonstick skillet over medium-high heat.

2. **Beat the eggs:** Put the eggs, water, and salt in a small mixing bowl. Using a fork, beat until combined but not frothy.

3. **Make the omelet:** Melt the butter in the skillet, and swirl it around to coat the bottom. Pour in the beaten eggs and reduce the heat to medium. Stir the eggs with a rubber spatula until you see small pieces of cooked eggs surrounded by liquid, then stop stirring. Cook for 30 to 45 seconds, or until the liquid is set and shiny.

4. **Fill the omelet:** Sprinkle the cheese over half the omelet.

5. **Fold the omelet:** Using a turner spatula, lift the half of the omelet that is not holding the filling and fold it over the filling. Slide the omelet out of the pan and onto a plate.

*Jazz It Up: There are endless options for fillings for your omelet. Try any of the following—just keep the total filling amount to about ⅓ cup—⅓ cup cooked meat like bacon, ham or sausage; ⅓ cup chopped and sautéed mushrooms, sweet red peppers, onions, spinach, or potatoes; ½ avocado, sliced; or 3 tablespoons salsa.*

PER SERVING: CALORIES: 330; TOTAL FAT: 29G; SODIUM: 645MG; CHOLESTEROL: 425MG; TOTAL CARBS: 2G; FIBER: 0G; SUGAR: 1G; PROTEIN: 18G

# Oatmeal

**SERVES** 2

**PREP TIME:** 5 minutes / **COOK TIME:** 10 minutes

Oatmeal is one of the quickest, healthiest, and most satisfying breakfasts to make. I love to make it on cold mornings. This recipe uses old-fashioned rolled oats. Old-fashioned oats have been steamed and then rolled.

**TOOLS AND EQUIPMENT**

medium saucepan

stirring spoon

**INGREDIENTS**

1 cup old-fashioned rolled oats

1 cup milk

1 cup water

⅛ teaspoon salt

**Make the oatmeal:** In a medium saucepan, combine the oats, milk, water, and salt. Bring to a boil over medium heat, then reduce the heat to low. Simmer, stirring occasionally, for 3 to 5 minutes, or until thickened. Remove from the heat. Let rest for 3 minutes.

*Another Idea:* *To make vegan oatmeal, substitute a nut milk like almond milk or coconut milk for the milk.*

PER SERVING: CALORIES: 211; TOTAL FAT: 5G; SODIUM: 207MG; CHOLESTEROL: 10MG; TOTAL CARBS: 33G; FIBER: 4G; SUGAR: 6G; PROTEIN: 9G

# French Toast

**SERVES** 2

**PREP TIME:** 5 minutes / **COOK TIME:** 10 minutes

French toast is easy to make. The secret is in the custard. You'll want to make sure you beat the eggs until they are a pale yellow. If you use day-old bread, or a bread like French bread or challah, try letting the custard soak into the bread a bit. Your French toast will have far more flavor and texture than if you simply coat the bread.

## TOOLS AND EQUIPMENT

shallow dish

fork

medium skillet

turner spatula

## INGREDIENTS

1 large egg

1 teaspoon pure
vanilla extract

½ teaspoon
ground cinnamon

¼ cup milk

4 slices bread

2 teaspoons butter

Maple syrup, for
serving (optional)

1. **Make the custard:** In a shallow dish, beat the egg, vanilla, and cinnamon. Stir in the milk.

2. **Dip the bread:** Using a fork, dip the bread in the egg mixture on one side, then turn and coat the other side.

3. **Cook:** In a medium skillet, melt the butter over medium heat. Once melted, place the custard-coated bread in the skillet and cook for about 3 minutes, or until browned. Using a turner spatula, flip the bread over and cook for about 3 minutes, or until golden brown. Drizzle maple syrup on top (if using).

*Pro Tip: Stale bread that is ¾ to 1 inch thick works best. Try using French bread, challah, or brioche for best results.*

*Pro Tip: If you haven't beaten your egg mixture enough, you will have streaks of cooked egg whites. You can avoid this by using a mesh strainer to strain your custard before coating the bread.*

PER SERVING: CALORIES: 231; TOTAL FAT: 9G; SODIUM: 341MG; CHOLESTEROL: 106MG; TOTAL CARBS: 26G; FIBER: 4G; SUGAR: 5G; PROTEIN: 12G

# Vegan French Toast

**SERVES** 2

**PREP TIME:** 5 minutes / **COOK TIME:** 20 minutes

This French toast uses no egg and a nondairy milk of your choice to make a great vegan meal. It's a delicious option for breakfast, snacking, or even dinner.

## TOOLS AND EQUIPMENT

medium mixing bowl

whisk

large skillet

fork

turner spatula

## INGREDIENTS

1½ cups nondairy milk, such as almond milk, soy milk, or coconut milk

2 tablespoons all-purpose flour

1 teaspoon sugar

1 teaspoon ground cinnamon

1 tablespoon vegetable oil

4 slices bread

1. **Make the batter:** In a medium mixing bowl, combine the nondairy milk, flour, sugar, and cinnamon. Whisk until well mixed.

2. **Make the French toast:** In a large skillet, heat the oil over medium-high heat. Using a fork, place 1 bread slice in the batter, then turn it over to coat the second side. Transfer the battered bread to the hot skillet and cook for about 3 minutes, or until golden brown. Using a turner spatula, flip the bread over and cook the second side for about 2 minutes, or until golden brown. Repeat with each slice of bread.

*Pro Tip: Try cooking more than one piece of French toast at a time in your skillet. As the French toast finishes cooking, use a spatula to move the French toast from the skillet to the serving plate.*

PER SERVING: CALORIES: 302; TOTAL FAT: 14G; SODIUM: 535MG; CHOLESTEROL: 0MG; TOTAL CARBS: 34G; FIBER: 6G; SUGAR: 5G; PROTEIN: 10G

# Pancakes

EXTRA QUICK, NUT-FREE, VEGETARIAN

**MAKES** 12 to 14 (3-inch) pancakes
**PREP TIME:** 5 minutes / **COOK TIME:** 15 minutes

Pancakes are easy to make for breakfast. You start with a batter, and when poured onto a hot griddle, it turns into fluffy cakes that pair well with fresh fruit, syrup, or jams. Pancakes turn out best when you don't overmix the dry and wet ingredients, so leave the batter lumpy.

## TOOLS AND EQUIPMENT

griddle

large mixing bowl

medium mixing bowl

whisk

stirring spoon

turner spatula

## INGREDIENTS

1 cup all-purpose flour

2 tablespoons sugar

2½ teaspoons
   baking powder

½ teaspoon baking soda

½ teaspoon salt

1 large egg

1¼ cups milk

3 tablespoons vegetable oil

3 tablespoons butter,
   melted, divided

1. **Prepare the batter:** Heat a griddle or large skillet over medium heat. In a large mixing bowl, stir together the flour, sugar, baking powder, baking soda, and salt. In a medium mixing bowl, whisk together the egg, milk, and oil. Pour the egg mixture all at once into the dry ingredients. Stir until just moistened (the batter will be lumpy).

2. **Make the pancakes:** Lightly grease the griddle with 1 tablespoon of butter. Make the pancakes in batches of 4. Pour ¼ cup batter per pancake onto the griddle, and cook for 1 to 2 minutes, or until the surface of the batter is bubbly and edges are slightly dry. Using a turner spatula, flip the pancakes over and cook for 1 to 2 minutes, or until golden. Repeat this entire step for the 2 remaining batches.

*Pro Tip:* *If you're cooking for the family, you can keep the finished pancakes warm while you continue cooking by placing finished pancakes in a single layer on a baking sheet in a 200-degree oven.*

PER SERVING (3 PANCAKES): CALORIES: 362; TOTAL FAT: 22G; SODIUM: 568MG; CHOLESTEROL: 76MG; TOTAL CARBS: 35G; FIBER: 1G; SUGAR: 10G; PROTEIN: 7G

# Blueberry Muffins

**MAKES** 12 regular muffins or 24 mini muffins
**PREP TIME:** 10 minutes / **COOK TIME:** 30 to 45 minutes

Sometimes life calls for a ridiculously easy blueberry muffin recipe. This quick and easy recipe results in moist, delicious muffins bursting with blueberries.

## TOOLS AND EQUIPMENT

muffin pan

large and medium mixing bowls

rubber spatula

oven mitts

wire cooling rack

## INGREDIENTS

Nonstick cooking spray

3 cups plus 2 tablespoons all-purpose flour

1 tablespoon baking powder

1 teaspoon salt

6 tablespoons unsalted butter, at room temperature

1¼ cups sugar

1 large egg

2 large egg yolks

1 teaspoon pure vanilla extract

1 cup milk

1¾ cups fresh blueberries

Sugar, for topping

1. **Prepare the batter:** Preheat the oven to 375°F. Grease a muffin pan, or coat the interior with nonstick cooking spray. In a large mixing bowl, sift together the flour, baking powder, and salt. In a medium mixing bowl, cream together the butter and sugar for about 3 minutes, or until fluffy. Add the egg, egg yolks, and vanilla. Mix until well combined. Beginning and ending with the flour mixture, alternately add the flour mixture and the milk, stirring well after each addition. Using a rubber spatula, gently fold in the berries.

2. **Bake:** Divide the batter among the cups of the muffin pan. Sprinkle sugar on top of the batter for each muffin. Transfer to the oven, and bake for 45 minutes (regular muffins) or 30 minutes (mini muffins), or until light golden and a toothpick inserted into the center of a muffin comes out clean. Remove from the oven. Let cool in the pan for 15 minutes, then turn out onto a wire cooling rack, and let cool completely.

*Pro Tip:* Instead of spraying the muffin pan directly, place a paper cupcake liner in each muffin cup, and spray them with nonstick spray.

PER SERVING (1 MUFFIN): CALORIES: 282; TOTAL FAT: 8G; SODIUM: 253MG; CHOLESTEROL: 67MG; TOTAL CARBS: 50G; FIBER: 1G; SUGAR: 24G; PROTEIN: 5G

# Banana Bread

NUT-FREE, VEGETARIAN

**MAKES** 1 (4½-by-8½-inch) loaf
**PREP TIME:** 10 minutes / **COOK TIME:** 1 hour

Once you've tried the basic version of this recipe, try it again with roasted bananas. Roast the unpeeled bananas at 250°F for 15 to 20 minutes, then complete the recipe as instructed.

## TOOLS AND EQUIPMENT

4½-by-8½-inch loaf pan
2 medium mixing bowls
stirring spoon
oven mitts
wire cooling rack

## INGREDIENTS

1 cup sugar
½ cup butter
3 ripe bananas, mashed
2 large eggs, beaten
1¼ cups flour
1 teaspoon baking soda
½ teaspoon salt

1. **Make the batter:** Preheat the oven to 350°F. Grease a 4½-by-8½-inch loaf pan. In a medium mixing bowl, cream together the sugar and butter. Add the bananas and eggs. Mix well. In a separate medium mixing bowl, combine the flour, baking soda, and salt. Mix until combined. Slowly add the dry ingredients to the banana mixture. Mix until the dry ingredients are moistened (do not overmix). Pour the batter into the loaf pan.

2. **Bake:** Place the loaf pan on the middle rack of the oven, and bake for 40 minutes. Cover the loaf with aluminum foil and bake for another 20 minutes, or until a toothpick inserted into the center comes out clean. Remove from the oven and run a knife around the edge of the pan. Turn the loaf out onto a wire cooling rack.

*Jazz It Up: Try a streusel-nut topping. In a small mixing bowl, combine 3 tablespoons packed brown sugar and 2 tablespoons all-purpose flour. Use a pastry blender or two knives to cut in 4 teaspoons of butter until the mixture looks like coarse crumbs. Add ¼ cup chopped walnuts if you like. Sprinkle the streusel topping over the batter before transferring to the oven.*

PER SERVING (½ OF LOAF): CALORIES: 216; TOTAL FAT: 9G; SODIUM: 268MG; CHOLESTEROL: 51MG; TOTAL CARBS: 33G; FIBER: 1G; SUGAR: 20G; PROTEIN: 3G

# Steak and Eggs

**SERVES** 1
**PREP TIME:** 5 minutes / **COOK TIME:** 8 minutes

This is a classic breakfast combination. Using a thin steak makes this meal come together quickly.

**TOOLS AND EQUIPMENT**

medium skillet

turner spatula

**INGREDIENTS**

1 tablespoon olive oil

½ teaspoon salt, divided

½ teaspoon freshly ground black pepper, divided

1 (4-ounce) thin steak

1 teaspoon butter

1 large egg

1. **Prepare the steak:** Season the steak with ¼ teaspoon of salt and ¼ teaspoon of pepper. In a medium skillet, heat the oil over medium heat. Add the steak and cook for 2 minutes, or until browned. Turn the steak over and cook for 2 minutes, or until the other side has browned. Transfer to a cutting board and let rest for about 5 minutes.

2. **Prepare the egg:** In the same skillet, melt the butter over medium heat. When the butter begins to sizzle, crack the egg into the butter. Cook for 1 to 2 minutes, or until the white begins to set. Season with the remaining ¼ teaspoon of salt and ¼ teaspoon of pepper. Using a turner spatula, flip the egg gently and cook for 1 minute. Transfer to the plate, add the steak, and enjoy.

*Pro Tip: Choose a hanger, chuck, or New York strip steak that is between ¼ and ½ inch in thickness.*

PER SERVING: CALORIES: 379; TOTAL FAT: 27G; SODIUM: 1260MG; CHOLESTEROL: 196MG; TOTAL CARBS: 1G; FIBER: 0G; SUGAR: 0G; PROTEIN: 32G

# Breakfast Tacos

**SERVES** 1

**PREP TIME:** 10 minutes / **COOK TIME:** 10 minutes

These breakfast tacos are loaded with your favorite breakfast staples—scrambled eggs, potato, bacon, and cheese. It's all bundled in soft taco shells, making breakfast a grab-and-go experience, with all the goodness breakfast should have.

## TOOLS AND EQUIPMENT

box grater

medium skillet

small mixing bowl

fork

rubber spatula

## INGREDIENTS

1 small red potato

1 tablespoon olive oil

½ teaspoon salt

¼ teaspoon freshly ground pepper

2 large eggs

¼ cup shredded Cheddar cheese

2 (8-inch) flour tortillas

2 slices of Easy Crispy Oven Bacon (see page 28) or cooked bacon

1. **Prepare the potato:** Grate the potato so it resembles raw hash browns. Blot with a paper towel to dry. In a medium skillet, heat the oil over medium heat. Once hot, add the potato and season with the salt and pepper. Cook for about 8 minutes, or until golden and beginning to brown.

2. **Beat the eggs:** Put the eggs in a small mixing bowl. Using a fork, beat until combined but not frothy.

3. **Make the egg:** Reduce the heat to low. Pour the eggs over the potato. Pull a rubber spatula from one end of the pan to the other for about 2 minutes, or until the eggs begin to form curds. Once the eggs begin to set but still show some runny areas, remove from the heat, and stir in the cheese.

4. **Make the tacos:** Divide the egg and potato mixture between the tortillas. Place 1 slice of bacon inside each tortilla.

*Jazz It Up:* Top Breakfast Tacos with sour cream, salsa, more cheese, black olives, or your favorite taco topping.

PER SERVING: CALORIES: 1002; TOTAL FAT: 57G; SODIUM: 2952MG; CHOLESTEROL: 443MG; TOTAL CARBS: 79G; FIBER: 7G; SUGAR: 4G; PROTEIN: 45G

# Green Chile Casserole

NUT-FREE

**SERVES** 6 to 8

**PREP TIME:** 15 minutes / **COOK TIME:** 40 minutes

This easy-to-make casserole is similar to a quiche, with a fluffy texture. It has just enough heat from the green chiles without being overpowering. Leftovers can easily be reheated.

## TOOLS AND EQUIPMENT

large skillet

9-by-13-inch baking pan

medium mixing bowl

whisk

oven mitts

## INGREDIENTS

1 cup chopped onion

1 pound ground turkey sausage

2 garlic cloves, minced

2 (4-ounce) cans whole green chilies, drained and seeded, divided

2 cups shredded Cheddar cheese, divided

4 large eggs

¼ cup all-purpose flour

1½ cups milk

½ teaspoon salt

Hot sauce

1. **Brown the sausage:** Preheat the oven to 350°F. Put the onion and sausage in a large skillet. Cook over medium heat, stirring occasionally, for about 5 minutes, or until the sausage has browned and the onions are translucent. Drain and safely discard the grease. Add the garlic to the skillet and stir.

2. **Prepare the casserole:** Lay the green chiles from the first can flat along the bottom of a 9-by-13-inch baking pan to cover. Top with 1½ cups of cheese. Add the meat mixture and lay the remaining chiles flat over the meat.

3. **Prepare the eggs:** In a medium mixing bowl, whisk the eggs with the flour until well combined. Add the milk, salt, and hot sauce. Whisk until combined. Pour the egg mixture into the baking pan.

4. **Bake:** Place the baking pan on the middle rack of the oven, and bake for 40 minutes, or until a knife inserted into the center comes out clean. Remove from the oven. Top with the remaining ½ cup of cheese, and let rest for 5 minutes.

*Pro Tip:* Using a hand mixer to beat the eggs will give the casserole a fluffier, even texture.

PER SERVING: CALORIES: 349; TOTAL FAT: 22G; SODIUM: 831MG; CHOLESTEROL: 205MG; TOTAL CARBS: 13G; FIBER: 2G; SUGAR: 6G; PROTEIN: 26G

# Cheesy Breakfast Bacon Muffins

**MAKES** 6 muffins
**PREP TIME:** 10 minutes / **COOK TIME:** 20 minutes

These muffins are versatile. We call them muffins, but you can also bake them in a greased 8-by-8-inch pan for 20 to 22 minutes to make a frittata. Or, add a thawed frozen pie crust to the pan before you pour in the egg mixture, and you'll have a quiche.

## TOOLS AND EQUIPMENT

muffin pan

medium mixing bowl

whisk

oven mitts

## INGREDIENTS

Nonstick cooking spray

6 large eggs

½ cup heavy cream

½ teaspoon salt

¼ teaspoon freshly ground pepper

½ cup shredded Cheddar cheese, divided

6 strips of cooked bacon, crumbled

½ cup bite-size broccoli florets

1 scallion, root trimmed and thinly sliced

¼ cup diced roasted red peppers

1. **Prepare the batter:** Preheat the oven to 375°F. Grease a muffin pan, or coat the interior with non-stick cooking spray. In a medium mixing bowl, combine the eggs with the heavy cream. Add the salt, pepper, and ¼ cup of cheese. Whisk until well blended. Fill each muffin cup three-fourths full with the egg mixture. Top with the bacon, broccoli, scallion, roasted red peppers, and remaining cheese.

2. **Bake:** Transfer the muffin pan to the oven, and bake for 18 to 20 minutes, or until the muffins have a slight rise and are golden brown on top. Remove from the oven. Let cool for 5 minutes.

*Store It:* You can store these muffins in the refrigerator in a resealable bag or sealed container for up to 3 days. Reheat in the microwave for 20 seconds for a quick snack.

PER SERVING: CALORIES: 287; TOTAL FAT: 24G; SODIUM: 790MG; CHOLESTEROL: 244MG; TOTAL CARBS: 3G; FIBER: 0G; SUGAR: 1G; PROTEIN: 16G

# Homemade Peanut Butter and Jelly Hand Pies

**MAKES** 4 hand pies
**PREP TIME:** 15 minutes / **COOK TIME:** 10 minutes

Make these homemade peanut butter and jelly hand pies and store them in a resealable sandwich bag for a quick breakfast.

## TOOLS AND EQUIPMENT

pizza cutter

small mixing bowl

fork

baking sheet

oven mitts

wire cooling rack

## INGREDIENTS

### FOR THE HAND PIES

1 (15-ounce) box of refrigerated rolled pie dough (2 pie crusts)

1 cup jam

1 tablespoon cornstarch

1 cup peanut butter

## TO MAKE THE HAND PIES

1. **Prepare the crust:** Preheat the oven to 400°F. Unroll 1 pie crust onto a cutting board. Using a pizza cutter, trim the curved parts from each circle of dough to make two roughly 10-by-10-inch squares. Then cut each square to make four 5-by-5-inch squares for each original circle of dough. Repeat with the other pie crust.

2. **Fill the crust:** In a small mixing bowl, mix together the jam with the cornstarch. Fill a resealable sandwich bag with the jam and cornstarch. Fill a second sandwich bag with peanut butter. Snip one corner of each bag to make a hole large enough to let the peanut butter and jelly out when you squeeze. Leaving a ¼-inch border all the way around, alternate thin strips of peanut butter and jelly on 4 squares.

3. **Seal the crust:** Wet your finger with a little water, and run it around the bare edges of the dough on 1 filled square. Add a top layer of pie crust, and using a fork, gently press the edges together to seal all the way around. Repeat with the remaining 3 filled squares. Transfer to a baking sheet.

## FOR THE GLAZE

1 cup powdered sugar

1 tablespoon milk

1 tablespoon jam

**4. Bake:** Transfer the baking sheet to the oven, and bake for 10 minutes, or until the crusts are light golden brown. Do not overbake, or you won't have any filling left inside. Remove from the oven. Transfer the hand pies to a wire cooling rack.

### TO MAKE THE GLAZE

**Glaze:** Once the hand pies are cool, in a small mixing bowl, combine the powdered sugar, milk, and jam. Mix until smooth. Spoon on top of the hand pies, and let dry. (Note: If you want to heat the hand pies, put them in the oven or the microwave. Do *not* put them in the toaster.)

*Pro Tip: If your glaze is too thick, add a little bit more milk. If the glaze starts to set while you are glazing the hand pies, put the bowl in the microwave for 5 to 10 seconds.*

*Another Idea: Experiment with fillings. My kids love using chocolate spread and marshmallow fluff or pie filling.*

PER SERVING: CALORIES: 1133; TOTAL FAT: 53G; SODIUM: 708MG; CHOLESTEROL: 10MG; TOTAL CARBS: 150G; FIBER: 5G; SUGAR: 38G; PROTEIN: 19G

# Chapter 4

# SNACKS AND SIDES

Sometimes the day calls for snacks. This chapter will help you prepare snacks and sides to impress. Treat yourself to easy Pull-Apart Pizza Bread (page 53) or serve some Potatoes au Gratin (page 65). Showcase your skills with a side of Green Beans with Bacon, Onion, and Garlic (page 62) or White Rice (page 58). Serve Homemade Salsa (page 50) with homemade Tortilla Chips (page 46), or set out appetizers like Artichoke-Spinach Dip (page 51) or Toasty Crab (page 52).

# Tortilla Chips

DAIRY-FREE, EXTRA QUICK, NUT-FREE, VEGAN

**SERVES** 6

**PREP TIME:** 10 minutes / **COOK TIME:** 10 minutes

Did you know you can make your own tortilla chips? It's so easy. You can use corn or flour tortillas. The size of your tortilla will affect the size of your chips, since you'll be cutting each tortilla into eight wedges. These chips are crunchy and go well with Homemade Salsa (page 50), or you can use them to make Nachos (page 47).

**TOOLS AND EQUIPMENT**

baking sheet

pizza cutter

oven mitts

**INGREDIENTS**

Nonstick cooking spray, for greasing

8 tortillas

Sea salt

1. **Prepare the tortillas:** Preheat the oven to 400°F. Coat a baking sheet with nonstick cooking spray. Using a pizza cutter, cut each tortilla in half, then turn and cut in half again. Now use the pizza cutter to cut an "X" in each tortilla. Arrange the tortilla wedges in a single layer on the baking sheet, so they don't overlap. Spray the wedges with cooking spray, and season with salt.

2. **Bake:** Place the baking sheet on the top rack of the oven, and bake for 5 minutes. Rotate the baking sheet, and bake for another 5 minutes, or until the chips are crispy. Remove from the oven. Let rest for 5 minutes.

*Store It: Store chips in a resealable bag for up to 4 days.*

*Jazz It Up: For a sweeter snack, try replacing the sea salt with cinnamon and sugar.*

PER SERVING: CALORIES: 76; TOTAL FAT: 2G; SODIUM: 22MG; CHOLESTEROL: 0MG; TOTAL CARBS: 14G; FIBER: 2G; SUGAR: 0G; PROTEIN: 2G

# Nachos

EXTRA QUICK, NUT-FREE, VEGETARIAN

**SERVES** 6
**PREP TIME:** 5 minutes / **COOK TIME:** 30 seconds

Nachos are a great snack and can be made into a meal. They are quick to make, and there are no set ingredients, so you can customize them to your liking. They are a great way to use up leftovers. Let your imagination run wild with the topping choices.

## TOOLS AND EQUIPMENT

box grater

2 large plates

## INGREDIENTS

1 (13-ounce) bag tortilla chips, or Tortilla Chips (p. 46)

1 pound Cheddar or Monterey Jack cheese

1. **Grate the cheese:** Grate the cheese onto a large plate.

2. **Make the nachos:** Put 1 layer of tortilla chips on a large microwave-safe plate. Top with half the cheese. Add another layer of tortilla chips, and top with the remaining cheese.

3. **Cook:** Microwave for 30 seconds. If your cheese has not quite melted, microwave for another 10 seconds. Repeat until the cheese has melted.

*Jazz It Up: Serve with your favorite toppings, like diced jalapeños, sliced black olives, diced avocado, sour cream, diced tomatoes, pico de gallo, diced onions, and diced grilled chicken or steak.*

*Pro Tip: Let your plate rest for 10 seconds in the microwave before adding more time. This will give the cheese time to melt.*

PER SERVING: CALORIES: 604; TOTAL FAT: 39G; SODIUM: 727MG; CHOLESTEROL: 79MG; TOTAL CARBS: 41G; FIBER: 3G; SUGAR: 1G; PROTEIN: 24G

# Hardboiled Eggs

**MAKES** 12 hardboiled eggs
**PREP TIME:** 5 minutes / **COOK TIME:** 11 minutes

There are so many possibilities with hardboiled eggs. You can eat one with a little salt and pepper, dress it up as a Deviled Egg (page 49), use it in a Cobb Salad (page 88), make egg salad, or slice it and use it as a garnish. To make softboiled eggs, reduce the cooking time to 7 minutes.

**TOOLS AND EQUIPMENT**

large pot with lid
slotted spoon
large mixing bowl

**INGREDIENTS**

12 large eggs
Ice cubes
Cold water

1. **Boil the eggs:** Put the eggs in a large pot, and cover with cold water by 1 inch. Bring to a boil over medium-high heat. Once boiling, turn off the heat, and cover. Let sit for 11 minutes. Meanwhile, fill a bowl with ice water.

2. **Shock the eggs:** Using a slotted spoon, immediately transfer the eggs to the bowl of ice water. Let sit for at least 5 minutes. Peel, and serve.

*Pro Tip: Every second counts when making hardboiled eggs. Fill a large mixing bowl with cold water, add ice cubes, and place in the freezer while your eggs cook. One minute before the timer goes off, place the ice water on the counter, where you will move the eggs from the hot water into the ice water to stop the eggs from cooking.*

PER SERVING: CALORIES: 70; TOTAL FAT: 5G; SODIUM: 65MG; CHOLESTEROL: 195MG; TOTAL CARBS: 1G; FIBER: 0G; SUGAR: 0G; PROTEIN: 6G

# Deviled Eggs

**MAKES** 12 deviled eggs

**PREP TIME:** 15 minutes

Deviled eggs are a classic snack. They are perfect for an Easter celebration or family gathering, but they are also delicious "just because."

## TOOLS AND EQUIPMENT

spoon

small mixing bowl

fork

platter

## INGREDIENTS

6 Hardboiled Eggs (page 48), shelled and cut in half

¼ cup mayonnaise

1 teaspoon white vinegar

1 teaspoon yellow mustard

⅛ teaspoon salt

Freshly ground black pepper

Paprika, for topping

1. **Prepare the eggs:** Gently scoop out the yolks from the eggs, and put them in a small mixing bowl. Put the egg whites on a platter.

2. **Prepare the filling:** Add the mayonnaise and vinegar to the bowl with the yolks. Using a fork, mash. Add the mustard and salt. Mix well. Season with pepper.

3. **Fill the eggs:** Spoon the filling into a resealable sandwich bag. Snip one corner of the bag to make a hole large enough to let filling out when you squeeze. Pipe the filling into each of the egg whites. Be sure to pipe in enough to make a small dome above the egg white. Season with paprika, and refrigerate until chilled.

*Jazz It Up:* For a flavor kick, try adding 1 or 2 drops of hot sauce or a tablespoon of dill pickle juice to the filling.

*Pro Tip:* You can prepare deviled eggs a day or two in advance. You can either assemble the deviled eggs, cover, and refrigerate; or keep the filling in the sandwich bag in the refrigerator, and snip the bag only when you're ready to fill the eggs. Refrigeration is a must until serving time.

PER SERVING (2 HALVES): CALORIES: 132; TOTAL FAT: 12G; SODIUM: 190MG; CHOLESTEROL: 189MG; TOTAL CARBS: 0G; FIBER: 0G; SUGAR: 0G; PROTEIN: 6G

# Homemade Salsa

DAIRY-FREE, EXTRA QUICK, GLUTEN-FREE, NUT-FREE, VEGAN

**SERVES** 8

**PREP TIME:** 10 minutes

Salsa is easy and quick and always a hit. If tomatoes are in season, substitute three medium fresh tomatoes for the canned tomatoes. You can also use this salsa to make a creamy dip (see Jazz It Up).

**TOOLS AND EQUIPMENT**

medium mixing bowl

**INGREDIENTS**

1 (14.5-ounce) can diced tomatoes

½ cup chopped fresh cilantro

¼ cup diced red onion

1 teaspoon sugar

¾ teaspoon ground cumin

½ teaspoon minced garlic

¼ teaspoon salt

1 jalapeño pepper, seeded and chopped (optional)

2 tablespoons freshly squeezed lemon or lime juice

**Make the salsa:** In a medium mixing bowl, combine the tomatoes, cilantro, onion, sugar, cumin, garlic, salt, and jalapeño (if using). Add the lemon juice in small increments, and taste as you go, since the citrus can overpower the salsa quickly.

*Store It: Place in an airtight container, and store in the refrigerator for up to 2 days.*

*Jazz It Up: Make a creamy salsa dip by adding 1 (8-ounce) package cream cheese at room temperature to ¼ cup salsa. Use an electric mixer to blend until smooth.*

PER SERVING: CALORIES: 95; TOTAL FAT: 0G; SODIUM: 426MG; CHOLESTEROL: 0MG; TOTAL CARBS: 19G; FIBER: 3G; SUGAR: 13G; PROTEIN: 3G

# Artichoke-Spinach Dip

**SERVES** 6

**PREP TIME:** 5 minutes / **COOK TIME:** 25 minutes

This is a cheesy artichoke-spinach dip that pairs well with toasted bread, crackers, or chips. Try substituting Parmesan for the Swiss cheese or mixing equal parts of Parmesan and Swiss for a different taste.

**TOOLS AND EQUIPMENT**

8-by-8-inch baking pan

large mixing bowl

spoon

oven mitts

**INGREDIENTS**

Nonstick cooking spray, for greasing

1 (8-ounce) jar artichoke hearts, drained and chopped

5 ounces frozen chopped spinach, thawed and drained well

2 cups shredded Swiss cheese

⅔ cup mayonnaise

1. **Prepare the pan:** Preheat the oven to 350°F. Coat the interior of an 8-by-8-inch baking pan with nonstick cooking spray.

2. **Mix the dip:** In a large mixing bowl, combine the artichoke hearts, spinach, cheese, and mayonnaise. Mix well.

3. **Bake the dip:** Scoop the dip into the baking pan. Transfer to the oven, and bake for 25 minutes, or until the edges bubble. Serve warm.

*Pro Tip:* To thaw frozen spinach in the microwave, put the amount of spinach you will need (in this case 5 ounces or ½ box) in a small microwave-safe bowl. Microwave the spinach on high for about 2 minutes, or until it becomes soft. Transfer to a colander lined with heavy-duty paper towels, then wrap the spinach and wring the moisture out. If you don't have a microwave, put the spinach straight into the (unlined) colander, and run warm water over it. Once all of the ice has melted, use your hands to squeeze the water out.

*Jazz It Up:* You can elevate the flavors of this dip by adding a splash or two of hot sauce in step 2.

PER SERVING: CALORIES: 311; TOTAL FAT: 27G; SODIUM: 273MG; CHOLESTEROL: 41MG; TOTAL CARBS: 7G; FIBER: 3G; SUGAR: 1G; PROTEIN: 12G

# Toasty Crab

**MAKES** 36 appetizers
**PREP TIME:** 5 minutes / **COOK TIME:** 2 minutes

This is an easy side or appetizer. It features crabmeat with a delicate bread crumb topping. If you're using it as a side, feel free to omit the toast and pour the mixture into a 5-by-6-inch casserole dish and broil for 4 minutes.

## TOOLS AND EQUIPMENT

medium mixing bowl

small mixing bowl

stirring spoon

baking sheet

pizza cutter

oven mitts

## INGREDIENTS

8 ounces crabmeat

1½ tablespoons mayonnaise

½ tablespoon prepared mustard

½ tablespoon freshly squeezed lemon juice

2 tablespoons grated Parmesan cheese

1 tablespoon bread crumbs

6 slices white bread, crusts removed, toasted

1. **Make the crab salad:** Position the top rack of the oven 3 inches under the broiler. Set the oven to broil, and preheat for 5 minutes. In a medium mixing bowl, combine the crabmeat, mayonnaise, mustard, and lemon juice. In a small mixing bowl, combine the cheese and bread crumbs.

2. **Bake:** Arrange the bread on a baking sheet in a single layer. Spread the crab mixture onto each slice. Sprinkle the bread crumb mixture on top. Using a pizza cutter or knife, cut each crab toast into 6 equal pieces. Place the baking sheet on the top rack of the oven, and broil for 2 minutes, or until browned. Remove from the oven.

*Pro Tip: Save time by using 2 (4.25-ounce) cans crabmeat, drained and picked over for shells.*

*Jazz It Up: Mince ½ small onion or 2 celery stalks, and add to the crab mixture in step 1 to give it more texture.*

PER SERVING (4): CALORIES: 91; TOTAL FAT: 3G; SODIUM: 123MG; CHOLESTEROL: 22MG; TOTAL CARBS: 9G; FIBER: 0G; SUGAR: 1G; PROTEIN: 7G

# Pull-Apart Pizza Bread

**SERVES** 6

**PREP TIME:** 15 minutes / **COOK TIME:** 30 minutes

This easy Pull-Apart Pizza Bread turns out delicious. It takes less than an hour to create—start to finish—and yields a crispy, cheesy, fun snack.

## TOOLS AND EQUIPMENT

pizza cutter

medium mixing bowl

Bundt pan

oven mitts

large plate

## INGREDIENTS

2 (13.8-ounce) tubes
  pizza dough

⅓ cup olive oil

2 cups shredded
  mozzarella cheese

1 cup shredded Parmesan
  cheese, plus more
  for garnish

½ cup fresh basil, shredded,
  plus more for garnish

2 tablespoons chopped
  fresh parsley

1 tablespoon
  Italian seasoning

½ teaspoon garlic powder

1 (5-ounce) bag mini
  pepperoni slices

1. **Make the bread:** Preheat the oven to 350°F. Using a pizza cutter, cut the pizza dough into 2-inch strips, then cut the strips into 2-inch squares. Transfer to a medium mixing bowl. Pour the oil over the dough. Add the mozzarella cheese, Parmesan cheese, basil, parsley, Italian seasoning, garlic powder, and pepperoni. Toss until well blended. Pour the pizza dough mixture into a Bundt pan.

2. **Bake:** Place the Bundt pan on the middle rack of the oven, and bake for 30 minutes, or until golden brown. Remove from the oven. Place a plate on top of the Bundt pan, and turn upside down. Garnish with additional Parmesan cheese and basil.

*Jazz It Up:* **Serve with a side of marinara sauce.**

PER SERVING: CALORIES: 919; TOTAL FAT: 68G; SODIUM: 1347MG; CHOLESTEROL: 59MG; TOTAL CARBS: 52G; FIBER: 4G; SUGAR: 1G; PROTEIN: 27G

# Corn on the Cob

EXTRA QUICK, GLUTEN-FREE, NUT-FREE, VEGETARIAN

**SERVES** 4

**PREP TIME:** 5 minutes / **COOK TIME:** 10 minutes

The fresher the corn, the better it will taste. When choosing ears of corn, look for green husks that are tightly wrapped around the cob. Pull the husk back a bit and look for bright, plump kernels arranged tightly in rows. The silk should be soft, moist, and pale golden in color. The more silk there is inside the husk, the better the corn. Finally, flip the corn upside down and make sure the stalk is still green.

**TOOLS AND EQUIPMENT**

large pot

tongs

colander

pastry brush

**INGREDIENTS**

2 tablespoons salt

4 ears fresh corn, shucked

4 tablespoons (½ stick) butter, melted

1. **Cook the corn:** Fill a large pot half full of water. Add the salt. Bring to a boil over high heat. Reduce the heat to medium-high, and using tongs, lower the corn into the boiling water. Return to a boil, and cook the corn for 5 minutes, or until tender.

2. **Serve:** Drain the corn, and use a pastry brush to coat the corn with the melted butter.

*Jazz It Up: Try making Mexican street corn. In a medium mixing bowl, combine ½ cup crumbled feta cheese, ⅓ cup mayonnaise, ⅓ cup sour cream, 1 tablespoon dried cilantro, 1 tablespoon lime juice, and 1 teaspoon chili powder. Stir until well combined. Drizzle over the cooked corn. This sauce also makes for a great vegetable dip and also tastes great mixed into rice or on top of baked potatoes.*

PER SERVING: CALORIES: 225; TOTAL FAT: 13G; SODIUM: 394MG; CHOLESTEROL: 31MG; TOTAL CARBS: 27G; FIBER: 4G; SUGAR: 5G; PROTEIN: 5G

# Baked Potatoes

**SERVES** 4

**PREP TIME:** 5 minutes / **COOK TIME:** 1 hour to 1 hour 15 minutes

Baked potatoes are versatile. They can be served as a classic with butter, or you can set up a baked potato bar with cheese, sour cream, bacon, chili, chives, or any of your other favorite toppings.

**TOOLS AND EQUIPMENT**

fork

oven mitts

**INGREDIENTS**

4 russet potatoes

Olive oil, for coating

Sea salt

1. **Prepare the potatoes:** Preheat the oven to 425°F. Using a fork, prick the potatoes all over to at least ⅛-inch depth (this relieves the pressure inside the potatoes by allowing the steam to escape as they cook). Coat each potato with oil, and season with salt.

2. **Bake:** Place the potatoes directly on the middle rack of the oven, and roast until the skin is crisp and the interior is soft when tested with a fork, 60 to 75 minutes. Remove from the oven.

*Pro Tip:* *When the potatoes are done, slice each potato down the center of one end, leaving ½ inch intact at the ends. Then, using an oven mitt, pinch the ends of the potatoes toward the center so the potatoes "open."*

*Pro Tip:* *The perfect internal temperature for a baked potato is 205°F. Use a digital cooking thermometer to help you determine when the potatoes are perfectly cooked.*

PER SERVING: CALORIES: 198; TOTAL FAT: 4G; SODIUM: 345MG; CHOLESTEROL: 0MG; TOTAL CARBS: 39G; FIBER: 3G; SUGAR: 1G; PROTEIN: 5G

# Baked French Fries

**SERVES** 4

**PREP TIME:** 10 minutes / **COOK TIME:** 30 minutes

These baked French fries are easy to make and don't require you to fry in hot grease that can splatter. They are crispy on the outside and fluffy on the inside. While French fries commonly use russet potatoes, you should try different varieties of potatoes for different flavors and textures. Yukon Gold potatoes are a good choice to start with. (You can make cleanup easy by covering the baking sheet with aluminum foil before cooking.)

**TOOLS AND EQUIPMENT**

baking sheet

oven mitts

tongs

**INGREDIENTS**

5 large potatoes, peeled

¼ cup plus 1 tablespoon vegetable oil

1¾ teaspoons salt

1. **Prepare the potatoes:** Preheat the oven to 450°F. Using a chef's knife, cut each potato into ½-inch slices (slabs) and then cut each slab into ½-inch sticks.

2. **Bake the fries:** Arrange the potato sticks on a baking sheet in a single layer. Pour the oil over the potatoes, and season with salt. Bake for 15 minutes. Remove from the oven. Using tongs, turn the fries over, keeping them in a single layer. Return to the oven, and bake for 15 minutes, or until crispy.

*Pro Tip: After cutting the potatoes, put them in a large mixing bowl filled with ice water, and let soak for 1 hour. Drain, then dry between paper towels. This will remove excess starch and help make your fries crispy.*

PER SERVING: CALORIES: 473; TOTAL FAT: 18G; SODIUM: 1047MG; CHOLESTEROL: 0MG; TOTAL CARBS: 73G; FIBER: 11G; SUGAR: 5G; PROTEIN: 8G

# Fluffy Mashed Potatoes

**SERVES** 4

**PREP TIME:** 10 minutes / **COOK TIME:** 20 minutes

Mashed potatoes are a great side dish to complement all kinds of meat, and they are easy to make. Russet potatoes are most commonly used for mashed potatoes, but try other varieties of potatoes like Yukon Gold or red potatoes for a change. Most people peel the potatoes before mashing them, but you can leave the skin on for a more rustic side dish.

**TOOLS AND EQUIPMENT**

vegetable peeler

medium saucepan with lid

fork

colander

potato masher

**INGREDIENTS**

9 medium potatoes, peeled

6 tablespoons
  (¾ stick) butter

¼ cup milk

½ teaspoon salt

¼ teaspoon freshly
  ground pepper

1. **Prepare the potatoes:** Using a chef's knife, quarter the potatoes. Put the potatoes in a medium saucepan, and add enough water to cover. Cover, and cook over medium-high heat for 20 minutes. Check for softness by pricking with a fork. Drain.

2. **Mash the potatoes:** Using a potato masher or electric mixer, thoroughly mash the potatoes until no lumps remain. Add the butter and milk. Stir until fluffy. Season with the salt and pepper.

*Jazz It Up:* Add 8 ounces diced cream cheese after the potatoes are mashed, and use an electric mixer to blend until smooth. Or, after you add the milk, try stirring in shredded Cheddar cheese or cooked bacon bits.

*Pro Tip:* Use heated butter and milk instead of cold. Put the butter and milk in a small microwave-safe bowl. Heat in the microwave in 15-second intervals, stirring in between, until the butter has melted. Add to the potatoes as directed.

PER SERVING: CALORIES: 491; TOTAL FAT: 18G; SODIUM: 449MG; CHOLESTEROL: 47MG; TOTAL CARBS: 76G; FIBER: 12G; SUGAR: 6G; PROTEIN: 9G

# White Rice

**SERVES** 4
**PREP TIME:** 5 minutes / **COOK TIME:** 15 minutes

White rice can be long grain, medium grain, or short grain. Common types of white rice are basmati and jasmine. Long grain holds its shape best. White rice has had the outer coating of the bran removed, whereas brown rice has only had the hull removed. Before cooking, you should pick over the rice and remove pieces that are blemished. Then, you should wash the rice by placing it in a strainer under cold running water.

**TOOLS AND EQUIPMENT**

medium saucepan with lid
fork

**INGREDIENTS**

1 cup white rice
2 cups water
1 teaspoon salt

1. **Make the rice:** In a medium saucepan, combine the rice, water, and salt. Bring to a boil over high heat. Reduce the heat to medium-low, cover, and simmer for 15 minutes, or until tender. Remove from the heat.

2. **Fluff:** Fluff the rice with a fork. Cover, and let rest for 10 minutes. This will redistribute the moisture and prevent mushy rice.

*Store It:* Store cooled leftovers covered in the refrigerator for up to 5 days or in the freezer for up to 1 month. Reheat in the microwave or on the stovetop with a little water until warm. It won't take much water; start with 1 tablespoon and add more water as needed.

*Pro Tip:* Rice is done when you pinch a rice kernel between the tips of two fingers and it feels tender.

*Jazz It Up:* For more flavor, try substituting chicken broth, beef broth, or vegetable broth for the water.

PER SERVING: CALORIES: 169; TOTAL FAT: 0G; SODIUM: 584MG; CHOLESTEROL: 0MG; TOTAL CARBS: 37G; FIBER: 1G; SUGAR: 0G; PROTEIN: 3G

# Coleslaw

**SERVES** 4
**PREP TIME:** 5 minutes

This basic coleslaw recipe is a classic, but you can customize it with a variety of vegetables and fruits to make it your own. The dressing is easy to make and tastes so much better than store-bought dressing. Try it and see if you don't agree.

## TOOLS AND EQUIPMENT

small mixing bowl

whisk

medium mixing bowl

## INGREDIENTS

½ cup mayonnaise

1½ tablespoons granulated sugar

1½ tablespoons apple cider vinegar

½ teaspoon salt

1 (14-ounce) package coleslaw mix

1. **Make the dressing:** In a small mixing bowl, whisk together the mayonnaise, sugar, vinegar, and salt until well combined and the sugar has dissolved.

2. **Make the coleslaw:** In a medium mixing bowl, combine the coleslaw mix and dressing. Mix and toss to evenly coat. Serve immediately.

*Pro Tip:* Do not add the dressing to the coleslaw mix until you're ready to serve.

*Another Idea:* Use 3 cups shredded green cabbage (also known as "cannonball cabbage") instead of the coleslaw mix. Once shredded, transfer to a large mixing bowl with 1 tablespoon salt, and let rest for 5 minutes. Drain any liquid and then proceed with the recipe as directed.

*Jazz It Up:* Try mixing in different ingredients for different textures and flavor, such as raisins, bacon, halved grapes, sunflower seeds, chopped carrots, or shredded apples.

PER SERVING: CALORIES: 223; TOTAL FAT: 20G; SODIUM: 489MG; CHOLESTEROL: 10MG; TOTAL CARBS: 10G; FIBER: 3G; SUGAR: 8G; PROTEIN: 1G

# Macaroni and Cheese

**SERVES** 8

**PREP TIME:** 5 minutes / **COOK TIME:** 15 minutes

Homemade macaroni and cheese is easy to make and tastes better than the kind in the box. It can be basic, or you can dress it up with bacon. It can be a side or become an entrée without much effort.

**TOOLS AND EQUIPMENT**

box grater

large pot

colander

small mixing bowl

medium saucepan

whisk

stirring spoon

**INGREDIENTS**

8 ounces elbow macaroni

2 tablespoons
all-purpose flour

½ teaspoon salt

¼ teaspoon garlic
powder (optional)

2 tablespoons
unsalted butter

1 cup whole milk

¼ cup sour cream

2 cups shredded
Cheddar cheese

1. **Cook the macaroni:** Cook the macaroni according to the package directions. Drain.

2. **Make the cheese sauce:** In a small mixing bowl, combine the flour, salt, and garlic powder (if using). In a medium saucepan, melt the butter over medium heat. Once the butter starts to bubble, add the flour mixture and whisk to combine. Cook for 1 minute, or until starting to turn golden brown. Add the milk slowly and continuously, whisking constantly until smooth. Whisk in the sour cream. Cook for 3 to 5 minutes, or until the sauce thickens (do not let it boil). Reduce the heat to low, add the cheese, and whisk until the cheese has melted. Remove from the heat.

3. **Add the macaroni:** Add the macaroni to the sauce, and stir until evenly coated. Let rest for 3 to 5 minutes.

*Another Idea: Use your favorite type of cheese for this recipe—Swiss, mozzarella, Jack—or any combination. Whatever kind you choose, grate it yourself rather than using pre-grated cheese. Pre-grated cheese has a coating of preservatives that prevents the cheese from melting well.*

PER SERVING: CALORIES: 285; TOTAL FAT: 15G; SODIUM: 361MG; CHOLESTEROL: 44MG; TOTAL CARBS: 25G; FIBER: 1G; SUGAR: 3G; PROTEIN: 12G

# Easy Sweet Corn Bread

NUT-FREE, VEGETARIAN

**SERVES** 8

**PREP TIME:** 10 minutes / **COOK TIME:** 50 minutes

This Easy Sweet Corn Bread recipe pairs perfectly with Great Northern Beans (page 111) and Vegetarian Chili (page 75). This recipe makes a lot of food. Eat the leftovers as a snack—trust me, it's hard to resist. Share with a neighbor, or store in the refrigerator. This recipe takes about an hour from start to finish.

## TOOLS AND EQUIPMENT

9-by-13-inch baking pan

large mixing bowl

stirring spoon

oven mitts

## INGREDIENTS

⅓ cup vegetable oil, plus more for greasing

2 (8.5-ounce) packages corn muffin mix

1 box yellow cake mix

5 large eggs

2 cups milk

1. **Prepare the batter:** Preheat the oven to 350°F. Grease a 9-by-13-inch baking pan. In a large mixing bowl, combine the corn muffin mix and cake mix. Add the eggs, milk, and oil. Stir just enough to moisten the dry ingredients. Pour the batter into the baking pan.

2. **Bake:** Place the baking pan on the middle rack of the oven, and bake for 45 to 50 minutes, or until a toothpick inserted into the center comes out clean. Remove from the oven.

*Jazz It Up:* Try adding a seeded and chopped jalapeño, ½ cup grated cheese, and 1 (15-ounce) can drained corn kernels for Southwestern flair.

*Pro Tip:* When a baking recipe provides a range of cooking time, always check on your dish after the lower end of the range has elapsed: If the toothpick comes out clean, pull the baking pan out of the oven. If the toothpick isn't clean, give it 5 more minutes and check again.

PER SERVING: CALORIES: 677; TOTAL FAT: 29G; SODIUM: 1015MG; CHOLESTEROL: 130MG; TOTAL CARBS: 95G; FIBER: 2G; SUGAR: 42G; PROTEIN: 12G

# Green Beans with Bacon, Onion, and Garlic

DAIRY-FREE, EXTRA QUICK, GLUTEN-FREE, NUT-FREE

**SERVES** 4
**PREP TIME:** 10 minutes / **COOK TIME:** 20 minutes

When selecting fresh green beans, look for crisp, slender green or yellow pods that snap. Wash them, and remove the ends and strings, if any. You can slice diagonally, using kitchen scissors to reduce the cooking time.

## TOOLS AND EQUIPMENT

medium saucepan

large skillet

colander

stirring spoon

## INGREDIENTS

1 pound fresh green beans, trimmed

3 quarts water

2 teaspoons salt

6 to 10 slices of Easy Crispy Oven Bacon (page 28) or cooked bacon

½ cup chopped yellow onion

2 tablespoons minced garlic

1. **Prepare the green beans:** In a medium saucepan, combine the green beans, water, and salt. Bring to a boil over medium heat. Cook for about 7 minutes, or until tender. Drain.

2. **Prepare the bacon and onions:** Meanwhile, chop the bacon into 1-inch pieces. Heat a large skillet over medium-low heat. Add the onion and garlic. Cook, stirring occasionally, for about 5 minutes, or until the onion is translucent.

3. **Make the dish:** Add the green beans to the skillet. Sauté, stirring occasionally, for 5 minutes, or until the onions and bacon are incorporated with the green beans. Serve hot.

*Jazz It Up:* Add 1½ cups diced, peeled tomatoes to the pan while cooking the onion.

*Pro Tip:* Fresh green beans should be firm after boiling, not limp. Before adding them to the bacon and onions, you can drain them and put them in ice water for 2 minutes to stop them from cooking so they stay crisp.

PER SERVING: CALORIES: 201; TOTAL FAT: 12G; SODIUM: 783MG; CHOLESTEROL: 31MG; TOTAL CARBS: 11G; FIBER: 4G; SUGAR: 2G; PROTEIN: 13G

# Broccoli-Corn Casserole

**SERVES** 6

**PREP TIME:** 10 minutes / **COOK TIME:** 1 hour 5 minutes

This casserole is easy to make, adds a pop of color on the plate, and is a great side dish with almost any main course. Try substituting cauliflower for the broccoli if you're looking for something different.

## TOOLS AND EQUIPMENT

fork

9-by-5-inch loaf pan

large saucepan

colander

large mixing bowl

2 small mixing bowls

oven mitts

## INGREDIENTS

1 large egg

Nonstick cooking spray

2 broccoli heads, broken into bite-size florets

¼ cup water

1 (14.75-ounce) can creamed corn

1 small onion, chopped

⅓ cup crushed saltine crackers, divided

⅛ teaspoon freshly ground pepper

2 tablespoons butter, melted

1. **Beat the egg:** Put the egg in a small mixing bowl. Using a fork, beat until combined but not frothy.

2. **Prepare the mixture:** Preheat the oven to 350°F. Coat the interior of a 9-by-5-inch loaf pan with nonstick cooking spray. In a large saucepan, combine the broccoli and water. Cook over medium heat for about 4 minutes, or until tender. Drain. In a large mixing bowl, combine the broccoli, corn, onion, ¼ cup of cracker crumbs, the egg, and pepper. Mix well. In a small mixing bowl, combine the butter and the remaining 1⅓ tablespoons of cracker crumbs until moist.

3. **Cook the casserole:** Pour the broccoli and corn mixture into the loaf pan. Sprinkle the butter and cracker crumb mixture on top of the casserole. Place on the middle rack of the oven, and bake for 1 hour, or until set. Remove from the oven.

*Pro Tip: Don't forget the stems. Peel and chop the broccoli stems, and cook them with the florets.*

PER SERVING: CALORIES: 159; TOTAL FAT: 6G; SODIUM: 320MG; CHOLESTEROL: 41MG; TOTAL CARBS: 25G; FIBER: 4G; SUGAR: 5G; PROTEIN: 6G

# Sweet Potato Casserole

**SERVES** 8

**PREP TIME:** 10 minutes / **COOK TIME:** 30 minutes

Most people only enjoy sweet potato casserole during the holidays, but it's so easy to make, you'll want to have it more often. You can top the casserole with marshmallows, pecans, or raisins to give it more flair.

**TOOLS AND EQUIPMENT**

paring knife

cutting board

9-by-11-inch baking pan

large mixing bowl

potato masher

electric mixer

oven mitts

**INGREDIENTS**

2 tablespoons butter, cut into small pieces, plus more for greasing

2 (15-ounce) cans sweet potatoes or yams

2 large eggs

¼ cup sugar

½ teaspoon ground cinnamon

½ teaspoon ground nutmeg

½ teaspoon ground allspice

1 cup milk

1. **Make the casserole:** Preheat the oven to 350°F. Grease a 9-by-11-inch baking pan with butter. In a large mixing bowl, mash the sweet potatoes, then add the eggs, sugar, cinnamon, nutmeg, and allspice. Beat with an electric mixer until combined. With the machine running, add the milk slowly until the mixture is smooth and soft.

2. **Bake:** Pour the sweet potato mixture into the baking pan, and dot with the butter. Place on the middle rack of the oven, and bake for 30 minutes, or until set.

*Pro Tip:* This easy sweet potato casserole can be prepared well ahead of time and refrigerated overnight to make meal prep easier. Remove it from the refrigerator 30 minutes prior to cooking, and increase the baking time to 40 minutes to heat through.

PER SERVING: CALORIES: 209; TOTAL FAT: 5G; SODIUM: 62MG; CHOLESTEROL: 57MG; TOTAL CARBS: 38G; FIBER: 5G; SUGAR: 8G; PROTEIN: 4G

# Potatoes au Gratin

**SERVES** 5

**PREP TIME:** 15 minutes / **COOK TIME:** 55 minutes

This is an easy recipe that requires few ingredients and yields a tasty dish perfect for a side, a potluck, or a small gathering of friends and family.

## TOOLS AND EQUIPMENT

vegetable peeler

chef's knife

cutting board

8-by-8-inch baking pan

medium saucepan

medium mixing bowl

whisk

oven mitts

## INGREDIENTS

Nonstick cooking spray, for greasing

5 medium potatoes, peeled and cut into thin rounds

2 cups shredded Cheddar cheese, divided

1 cup beef stock

¾ cup half-and-half or 2 percent milk

1. **Prepare the potatoes:** Preheat the oven to 400°F. Lightly coat an 8-by-8-inch baking pan with nonstick cooking spray. Put the potatoes in a medium saucepan, and add enough water to cover. Simmer for about 8 minutes, or until tender. Drain. In the baking pan, create alternating layers of the potatoes and 1¾ cups of cheese.

2. **Make the liquid:** In a medium mixing bowl, whisk together the beef stock and half-and-half until well combined. Pour the liquid over the potatoes. Sprinkle the remaining ¼ cup of cheese on top.

3. **Bake:** Place the baking pan on the middle rack of the oven, and bake for 45 minutes, or until the edges bubble and the top is deep golden brown. Remove from the oven. Let rest for 5 minutes before serving.

*Pro Tip: To save time, use a fork to poke holes in the potatoes, and microwave for 5 minutes. Let rest in the microwave for 5 minutes, then slice into rounds.*

*Jazz It Up: Add 1 tablespoon whole-grain mustard to the beef broth and half-and-half in step 2.*

PER SERVING: CALORIES: 387; TOTAL FAT: 20G; SODIUM: 434MG; CHOLESTEROL: 61MG; TOTAL CARBS: 36G; FIBER: 5G; SUGAR: 3G; PROTEIN: 17G

ALMOST HOMEMADE TOMATO SOUP, PAGE 72

## Chapter 5

# SOUPS AND SALADS

Whether you want to bring the Macaroni Salad (page 84) to the next family gathering or make a warm pot of Zuppa Toscana (page 79) on a cold day for lunch, you'll find a recipe in this chapter to satisfy your cravings. Serve Beef Taco Layer Salad (page 87) as a meal or a dip, or perfect the Chicken Soup (page 69) and share it with a friend who is feeling under the weather. Chapter 5 is full of satisfying recipes for every occasion.

# Easy Ramen Noodles

DAIRY-FREE, EXTRA QUICK, NUT-FREE, VEGETARIAN

**SERVES** 2

**PREP TIME:** 5 minutes / **COOK TIME:** 10 minutes

Ramen noodles are a staple. They're a convenient go-to for a quick meal. This recipe elevates the ramen experience.

**TOOLS AND EQUIPMENT**

medium saucepan

stirring spoon

**INGREDIENTS**

1 tablespoon vegetable oil

1 garlic clove, minced

1 scallion, root trimmed and green and white parts sliced

¼ teaspoon hot sauce

3 cups vegetable broth

2 teaspoons soy sauce

½ cup water

1 (12-ounce) package ramen noodles, seasoning packet discarded

1. **Prepare the vegetables:** In a medium saucepan, heat the oil over medium heat. Add the garlic, scallion, and hot sauce. Cook for 2 minutes, or until the scallion begins to soften and the white part becomes translucent.

2. **Make the broth:** Add the vegetable broth, soy sauce, and water. Increase the heat to medium-high, and bring to a boil. Add the noodles, and cook for 3 minutes, or until tender. Ladle the soup into 2 serving bowls.

*Jazz It Up: Slice a hardboiled egg, and top each bowl with half the slices before serving.*

PER SERVING: CALORIES: 470; TOTAL FAT: 21G; SODIUM: 1322MG; CHOLESTEROL: 0MG; TOTAL CARBS: 58G; FIBER: 4G; SUGAR: 3G; PROTEIN: 11G

# Chicken Soup

**SERVES** 6

**PREP TIME:** 5 minutes / **COOK TIME:** 20 minutes

When my kids were little, I made this soup often, not only when they were feeling under the weather, but also when they brought friends home with them after school and I didn't know how many kids to expect. To stretch this soup, you can just add more vegetables. To speed up the cooking time, you can also use leftover cooked chicken or canned chicken.

## TOOLS AND EQUIPMENT

chef's knife

cutting board

medium skillet

stirring spoon

large saucepan

## INGREDIENTS

2 tablespoons butter

½ yellow onion, chopped

1 boneless skinless chicken breast, chopped

1 (32-ounce) container chicken broth

2 (14.5-ounce) cans mixed vegetables

1 bay leaf

1. **Cook the chicken:** In a medium skillet, melt the butter over medium heat. Add the onion and chicken. Sauté for about 7 minutes, or until the chicken has cooked through and the onion is translucent.

2. **Make the soup:** In a large saucepan, combine the chicken broth, chicken, onion, vegetables, and bay leaf. Bring to a boil over medium-high heat. Reduce the heat to medium-low, and simmer for 10 minutes, or until heated through. Remove from the heat. Discard the bay leaf before serving.

*Jazz It Up:* Add 2 cups cooked pasta, such as egg noodles or elbow macaroni, for chicken noodle soup.

PER SERVING: CALORIES: 164; TOTAL FAT: 5G; SODIUM: 557MG; CHOLESTEROL: 26MG; TOTAL CARBS: 18G; FIBER: 3G; SUGAR: 5G; PROTEIN: 13G

# Chicken Tortilla Soup

**SERVES** 4

**PREP TIME:** 10 minutes / **COOK TIME:** 20 minutes

Chicken Tortilla Soup is one of my favorite comfort foods. It's a great way to use up leftover chicken, or substitute turkey for the chicken to give Thanksgiving leftovers a new spin. Garnish this dish with some chopped fresh cilantro for a fresh burst of flavor.

**TOOLS AND EQUIPMENT**

large saucepan with lid
stirring spoon

**INGREDIENTS**

1 tablespoon vegetable oil

1 small onion, chopped

2 garlic cloves, minced

1 medium jalapeño pepper, seeded and chopped

5 (14.5-ounce) cans chicken broth

2 (14.5-ounce) cans diced tomatoes

1 pound cooked chicken, shredded

½ teaspoon salt

1 ripe medium avocado

Corn tortilla chips

½ cup shredded Monterey Jack cheese

1 lime, cut into wedges

1. **Prepare the vegetables:** In a large saucepan, heat the oil over medium-high heat. Add the onion, and cook, stirring frequently, for 2 minutes, or until starting to turn translucent. Add the garlic and jalapeño. Cook, stirring frequently, for 2 to 3 minutes, or until fragrant.

2. **Make the soup:** Stir in the broth, tomatoes, chicken, and salt. Bring to a boil. Reduce the heat to medium-low, cover, and simmer for 15 minutes, or until the chicken is heated through.

3. **Serve:** To serve, peel and pit the avocado. Cut it into 1-inch slices. Divide the tortilla chips among 4 serving bowls. Ladle the soup into each bowl. Top each serving with avocado and cheese; garnish with additional tortilla chips. Serve with lime wedges.

*Pro Tip: Don't add the corn chips to the soup until just before serving. They are for texture and garnish.*

PER SERVING: CALORIES: 479; TOTAL FAT: 51G; SODIUM: 732MG; CHOLESTEROL: 153MG; TOTAL CARBS: 21G; FIBER: 7G; SUGAR: 7G; PROTEIN: 51G

# Chicken and Dumplings

**SERVES** 6

**PREP TIME:** 15 minutes / **COOK TIME:** 25 minutes

This chicken and dumplings recipe is a filling and comforting soup. The dumplings are made with prepackaged biscuit dough that is cooked right in the soup itself.

## TOOLS AND EQUIPMENT

vegetable peeler

large saucepan with lid

medium mixing bowl

whisk

## INGREDIENTS

2 tablespoons butter

½ yellow onion, finely chopped

1 cup chopped carrots

2 celery stalks, chopped

1 pound cooked chicken, chopped

4 cups chicken broth

1 (10.5-ounce) can condensed cream of chicken soup

¼ teaspoon freshly ground pepper

1 cup frozen peas

1 tablespoon all-purpose flour

1 (16.3-ounce) tube refrigerated biscuits

1. **Prepare the chicken and vegetables:** In a large saucepan, melt the butter over medium-high heat. Add the onion, carrots, celery, and chicken. Cook for about 5 minutes, or until the onion is translucent.

2. **Make the soup:** In a medium mixing bowl, whisk together the broth, soup, and pepper. Add to the chicken and vegetables. Bring to a boil. Reduce the heat to medium-low. Add the peas, cover, and simmer, stirring occasionally, for 5 minutes.

3. **Make the dumplings:** Sprinkle the flour on a cutting board. Press each biscuit with the palm of your clean hand until it is ¼ inch thick. Cut the biscuits into quarters. One at a time, drop a piece of biscuit into the soup. Cover and simmer, stirring occasionally, for 15 minutes, or until the biscuits are puffy and cooked through. Remove from the heat.

*Pro Tip:* *Before covering the dumplings, give them a quick stir. This will help envelop them in the broth.*

PER SERVING: CALORIES: 417; TOTAL FAT: 11G; SODIUM: 1069MG; CHOLESTEROL: 87MG; TOTAL CARBS: 46G; FIBER: 4G; SUGAR: 8G; PROTEIN: 33G

# Almost Homemade Tomato Soup

**SERVES** 4

**PREP TIME:** 5 minutes / **COOK TIME:** 10 minutes

This easy creamy tomato soup recipe is "almost" homemade. It starts with a jar of spaghetti sauce and transforms into a delicious soup that is pure comfort food. I think it's just as easy to make as opening a can, and my family enjoys it far more. Serve with a Grilled Cheese Sandwich (page 93) for a great dinner option.

## TOOLS AND EQUIPMENT

medium saucepan

whisk

## INGREDIENTS

1 (26-ounce) jar tomato and basil spaghetti sauce

3 cups heavy cream

½ cup sugar

1½ teaspoons Worcestershire sauce

Fresh basil, shredded, for topping

1. **Make the soup:** Pour the spaghetti sauce into a medium saucepan. Blend in the cream. Add the sugar and Worcestershire sauce. Whisk to combine. Heat over medium heat until warm and the sugar has dissolved (do not boil). Remove from the heat.

2. **Serve:** Ladle the soup into 4 bowls and top with basil.

*Jazz It Up:* Toast a piece of hearty bread (sourdough works well), tear it into bite-size pieces, and place in the center of each bowl for an elegant touch.

*Another Idea:* For a smoother soup, purée the spaghetti sauce in the blender before adding it to the saucepan.

PER SERVING: CALORIES: 756; TOTAL FAT: 66G; SODIUM: 1054MG; CHOLESTEROL: 245MG; TOTAL CARBS: 40G; FIBER: 3G; SUGAR: 33G; PROTEIN: 6G

# Vegetable Soup

**SERVES** 2

**PREP TIME:** 10 minutes / **COOK TIME:** 20 minutes

A cup of warm soup goes a long way. This Vegetable Soup uses fresh ingredients and comes together quickly. It's perfect for warming you up and taking the chill out of a cold day. Consider this a basic foundation for your own vegetable soup. You can add your favorite vegetables (frozen or fresh), and you can add leftover meat such as chicken or beef.

## TOOLS AND EQUIPMENT

vegetable peeler

medium saucepan

stirring spoon

## INGREDIENTS

1 teaspoon olive oil

½ small onion, chopped

1 celery stalk, chopped

1 large carrot, chopped

½ garlic clove, minced

1 cup vegetable broth

1 (14.5-ounce) can diced tomatoes with Italian seasonings

¼ cup cooked elbow pasta

½ teaspoon salt

¼ teaspoon freshly ground pepper

1. **Prepare the vegetables:** In a medium saucepan, heat the oil over medium heat. Add the onion, celery, and carrot. Cook, stirring occasionally, for 10 minutes, or until the vegetables are tender. Add the garlic, and stir.

2. **Make the soup:** Add the broth, tomatoes, and pasta. Season with the salt and pepper. Simmer for about 10 minutes, or until heated through. Remove from the heat.

*Jazz It Up: Dress up your soup bowl with a sprig or two of parsley, Parmesan cheese, or a spritz of freshly squeezed lemon juice. They each add something wonderful to this vegetable soup.*

PER SERVING: CALORIES: 135; TOTAL FAT: 3G; SODIUM: 1124MG; CHOLESTEROL: 0MG; TOTAL CARBS: 23G; FIBER: 4G; SUGAR: 10G; PROTEIN: 3G

# Broccoli-Cheese Soup

**SERVES** 4

**PREP TIME:** 10 minutes / **COOK TIME:** 30 minutes

This soup is perfect for crisp fall and chilly winter weather. It has a creamy base and the rich flavor of Cheddar cheese, complemented with pieces of broccoli and carrots. It comes together in about 30 minutes for a fast meal that will warm you up. Serve with French bread or add some croutons for garnish.

## TOOLS AND EQUIPMENT

vegetable peeler

box grater

large saucepan

stirring spoon

whisk

## INGREDIENTS

2 tablespoons butter

½ cup chopped
  yellow onion

2 tablespoons
  all-purpose flour

3 cups milk

1 cup vegetable broth

2 cups chopped
  cooked broccoli

1 cup julienned carrots

2 cups shredded
  Cheddar cheese

Salt

Freshly ground
  black pepper

½ teaspoon sour cream

1. **Make a roux:** In a large saucepan, melt the butter over medium heat. Add the onion. Cook for about 5 minutes, or until tender. Stir in the flour. Cook for about 1 minute, then slowly add the milk and vegetable broth, about ¼ cup at a time, whisking until thickened and smooth.

2. **Make the soup:** Add the broccoli and carrots. Simmer for about 10 minutes, or until heated through and the flavors meld. Stir in the cheese, and cook for 10 minutes, or until fully melted and blended through. Season with salt and pepper. Remove from the heat.

3. **Serve:** Stir in the sour cream, and serve.

*Helpful Hint: To julienne carrots, cut off a thin slice of the carrot on one side lengthwise so you can lay the carrot flat on the cutting board and it is stable. Cut the carrot crosswise into thirds. For each third, cut ⅛-inch lengthwise slices, then cut each slice into ⅛-inch-wide strips, or "matchsticks." If you don't have time to julienne the carrots, you can use grated carrot instead.*

PER SERVING: CALORIES: 424; TOTAL FAT: 29G; SODIUM: 687MG; CHOLESTEROL: 90MG; TOTAL CARBS: 21G; FIBER: 3G; SUGAR: 12G; PROTEIN: 22G

# Vegetarian Chili

**SERVES** 6

**PREP TIME:** 5 minutes / **COOK TIME:** 40 minutes

Chili is comfort food. It has a tangy tomato base and a lot of texture. This vegetarian chili isn't as heavy as chili with meat, yet still offers the flavors you expect from a hearty chili. It's even better the next day. Try using leftovers on baked potatoes.

## TOOLS AND EQUIPMENT

can opener

large saucepan

stirring spoon

## INGREDIENTS

2 tablespoons vegetable oil

1 yellow onion, chopped

2 (14.5-ounce) cans diced tomatoes, chopped

2 (15-ounce) cans dark red kidney beans, drained and rinsed

2 tablespoons chili powder

2 teaspoons salt

1. **Prepare the chili:** In a large saucepan, heat the oil over medium heat. Add the onion, and cook for about 5 minutes, or until translucent. Add the tomatoes with their liquid, beans, chili powder, and salt.

2. **Simmer:** Simmer, stirring occasionally, for 30 minutes, or until heated through and the flavors meld. Remove from the heat.

*Jazz It Up:* *Add ¼ teaspoon red pepper flakes if you want to kick up the heat.*

*Another Idea:* *If you want the chili to be a little thicker, try adding ⅛ cup of toasted wheat germ after simmering for 30 minutes, and simmer for another 5 minutes to thicken.*

PER SERVING: CALORIES: 194; TOTAL FAT: 6G; SODIUM: 810MG; CHOLESTEROL: 0MG; TOTAL CARBS: 29G; FIBER: 9G; SUGAR: 5G; PROTEIN: 9G

# Chicken Chili

**SERVES** 2

**PREP TIME:** 10 minutes / **COOK TIME:** 30 minutes

This is an easy chili perfect for a crisp fall evening or to warm the soul during winter. Feel free to leave the kidney beans out if you are from the school of thought that beans don't belong in chili.

**TOOLS AND EQUIPMENT**

can opener

pastry brush

8-by-8-inch baking pan

cooking thermometer

medium skillet

stirring spoon

oven mitts

**INGREDIENTS**

1 chicken breast

2 tablespoons olive
  oil, divided

½ teaspoon salt, plus more
  as needed

Freshly ground
  black pepper

1. **Bake the chicken:** Preheat the oven to 400°F. Using a pastry brush, coat the chicken with 1 tablespoon of oil, then season with the salt and pepper. Put the chicken in an 8-by-8-inch baking pan. Transfer to the oven, and bake for 15 to 18 minutes, or until the internal temperature reaches 165°F. Remove from the oven. Once cool enough to handle, transfer the chicken to a cutting board and chop.

2. **Prepare the vegetables:** Meanwhile, in a medium skillet, heat the remaining 1 tablespoon of oil over medium-low heat. Add the onion, and cook for 7 to 9 minutes, or until translucent. Add the garlic, and cook, stirring, for 30 seconds, or until fragrant. Add the bell pepper, basil, chili powder, cumin, and salt. Cook, stirring, for 1 minute or until fragrant. Add the diced tomatoes. Bring to a boil, then reduce the heat to medium-low. Simmer for 15 minutes, or until heated through and the flavors meld.

½ small onion, chopped

1 garlic clove, minced

1 small red bell
pepper, diced

½ teaspoon dried basil

¼ teaspoon chili powder

¼ teaspoon ground cumin

1 (15-ounce) can
diced tomatoes

1 (15-ounce) can red kidney
beans, drained and rinsed

¼ cup shredded Cheddar
cheese (optional)

Sour cream, for
topping (optional)

3. **Make the chili:** Add the chicken and beans. Simmer, stirring, for 5 minutes, or until heated through. Ladle the chili into a bowl, and top with cheese (if using) and sour cream (if using).

*Pro Tip: Try using leftover chicken or a precooked chicken breast if you're pressed for time.*

*Jazz It Up: Add 1 tablespoon diced green chiles for a twist on the flavor.*

PER SERVING: CALORIES: 453; TOTAL FAT: 18G; SODIUM: 644MG; CHOLESTEROL: 54MG; TOTAL CARBS: 46G; FIBER: 14G; SUGAR: 10G; PROTEIN: 32G

# Shrimp and Avocado Soup

**SERVES** 4

**PREP TIME:** 10 minutes / **COOK TIME:** 15 minutes

This easy Shrimp and Avocado Soup recipe will warm you through the winter and is still light enough to eat through the summer. It is filled with whole foods and all the flavors of a beach retreat.

## TOOLS AND EQUIPMENT

box grater

medium pot

stirring spoon

## INGREDIENTS

8 cups chicken broth

1 onion, chopped

1 jalapeño pepper, chopped

2 garlic cloves, chopped

2 teaspoons lime zest

1 teaspoon cumin

28 shrimp, peeled

Juice of 2 limes

½ teaspoon salt

Dash hot sauce

1 cup tomatoes, chopped

2 avocados, peeled, pitted, and chopped

½ cup cilantro, for garnish (optional)

2 limes cut into wedges, for serving (optional)

**Make the soup:** In a medium pot, combine the chicken broth, onion, jalapeño, garlic, lime zest, and cumin. Simmer for 10 minutes, or until heated through and the flavors meld. Add the shrimp, lime juice, salt, and hot sauce. Cook for 3 minutes, or until the shrimp turn pink. Remove from the heat. Stir in the tomatoes and avocados. Garnish with the cilantro (if using) and serve with the lime wedges (if using).

*Pro Tip:* *For easy juicing, place the limes in the microwave for 10 seconds. Then, roll the lime on the counter under the palm of your hand. Cut in half crosswise, and juice.*

PER SERVING: CALORIES: 337; TOTAL FAT: 45G; SODIUM: 1266MG; CHOLESTEROL: 214MG; TOTAL CARBS: 15G; FIBER: 7G; SUGAR: 3G; PROTEIN: 33G

# Zuppa Toscana

NUT-FREE

**SERVES** 6

**PREP TIME:** 15 minutes / **COOK TIME:** 30 minutes

Zuppa Toscana, which means "Tuscan-style soup," is an Italian soup made with sausage, potatoes, kale, and a creamy broth. It is full of textures, flavors, and hardy goodness.

## TOOLS AND EQUIPMENT

medium skillet

large pot

stirring spoon

## INGREDIENTS

1 pound bulk
  Italian sausage

¼ to ½ teaspoon red
  pepper flakes

1 cup chopped onion

2 large russet potatoes,
  halved and cut into
  ¼-inch slices

1 (14.5-ounce) can
  chicken broth

4 cups water

2 garlic cloves, minced

⅓ cup cooked bacon pieces

Salt

Freshly ground
  black pepper

2 cups chopped kale

1 cup heavy cream

1. **Prepare the meat and vegetables:** In a medium skillet, cook the sausage over medium heat for about 5 minutes, or until browned. Add the red pepper flakes. Cook the sausage for about another 2 minutes on each side, or until cooked through. Remove from the heat. In a large pot, combine the onion, potatoes, chicken broth, water, and garlic. Bring to a boil over medium heat. Cook for about 10 minutes, or until the potatoes have cooked through.

2. **Make the soup:** Stir in the sausage and bacon. Season with salt and pepper. Simmer for 10 minutes, or until the flavors meld, then reduce the heat to low. Add the kale and cream. Cook for about 10 minutes, or until heated through (do not boil). Remove from the heat.

3. **Serve:** Ladle the soup into 6 bowls, and serve.

*Jazz It Up: Try using hot Italian sausage to give this soup a spicy kick. I like to mix hot and mild Italian sausage.*

*Store It: Leftovers should be refrigerated and used within 3 days.*

PER SERVING: CALORIES: 434; TOTAL FAT: 34G; SODIUM: 509MG; CHOLESTEROL: 119MG; TOTAL CARBS: 25G; FIBER: 4G; SUGAR: 2G; PROTEIN: 17G

# French Onion Soup

NUT-FREE

**SERVES** 4

**PREP TIME:** 15 minutes / **COOK TIME:** 1 hour 35 minutes

There is something elegant about French Onion Soup. The ingredients are basic, yet it has such a complex, deep flavor. Great French onion soup comes down to properly caramelized onions, which take some time but are so important to the flavor.

## TOOLS AND EQUIPMENT

5- to 6-quart pot

stirring spoon

medium saucepan with lid

baking sheet

pastry brush

oven mitts

## INGREDIENTS

4 cups thinly sliced onions

8 tablespoons (1 stick) butter, divided

1 teaspoon sugar

¼ teaspoon freshly ground pepper

6 cups beef stock

1 tablespoon salt

1. **Caramelize the onions:** In a 5- to 6-quart heavy-bottomed pot, melt 4 tablespoons of butter over medium heat. Add the onions. Toss to coat them with the butter. Cook, stirring often, for 15 to 20 minutes, or until soft. Increase the heat to medium-high. Add the remaining 4 tablespoons of butter and the sugar. Cook, stirring often, for about 15 minutes, or until the onions start to brown. Season with the pepper.

2. **Make the broth:** In a medium saucepan, bring the beef stock to a boil over medium heat. Add the onions and salt. Cover, reduce the heat to medium-low, and simmer gently for 1 hour, or until the flavors meld. Remove from the heat.

3. **Prepare the bread:** About 15 minutes before the broth is finished, preheat the oven to 450°F. Line a baking sheet with aluminum foil. Put the bread on the baking sheet, and brush with ¾ tablespoon of oil. Place the baking sheet on the middle rack of the oven, and toast for 5 to 7 minutes, or until lightly browned. Turn the bread over, brush with the remaining ¾ tablespoon of oil, and top with Parmesan cheese. Return to the oven, and cook for 2 minutes, or until the bread is toasted. Remove from the oven.

4 (1-inch thick) slices
French bread

1½ tablespoons olive
oil, divided

¼ cup grated
Parmesan cheese

1½ cups shredded
Gruyère cheese

**4. Serve:** Place 1 piece of toast in each of 4 soup bowls, and ladle the soup over the bread. Once the bread rises to the top of the bowl, sprinkle with the Gruyère cheese.

*Pro Tip:* *Let your onions cook slowly. Cooking them slowly over lower heat allows their sugars to release and create a rich, golden caramelization.*

PER SERVING: CALORIES: 590; TOTAL FAT: 42G; SODIUM: 2123MG; CHOLESTEROL: 103MG; TOTAL CARBS: 32G; FIBER: 3G; SUGAR: 7G; PROTEIN: 24G

# Cucumber Salad

**SERVES** 2
**PREP TIME:** 10 minutes

This cucumber salad is a great recipe for practicing your knife skills. You can use any type of cucumber and tomato. Try using ½ cup cherry tomatoes and slice them in half or a diced Roma tomato, which is less juicy. To maximize the flavors, let this salad rest in the refrigerator, covered, for 30 minutes.

## TOOLS AND EQUIPMENT

vegetable peeler

chef's knife

paring knife

medium mixing bowl

## INGREDIENTS

1 cucumber, peeled
  and chopped

1 tomato, cored and diced

1 small red onion,
  coarsely chopped

½ cup vinaigrette dressing
  (page 89)

Sesame seeds, for
  topping (optional)

**Make the salad:** In a medium mixing bowl, combine the cucumber, tomato, and onion. Add the vinaigrette dressing, and toss to coat. Top with sesame seeds (if using).

*Pro Tip: Always rinse onions in cold water after slicing. It reduces the residue left on them that causes bad breath.*

PER SERVING: CALORIES: 162; TOTAL FAT: 9G; SODIUM: 606MG; CHOLESTEROL: 0MG; TOTAL CARBS: 16G; FIBER: 2G; SUGAR: 11G; PROTEIN: 2G

# Tuna Salad

**SERVES** 4

**PREP TIME:** 5 minutes

Tuna Salad is delicious on bread, spread onto crackers, or scooped into lettuce cups. Some people like the basic version with just tuna and mayonnaise, while others prefer more crunch to their salad. It's all personal preference. Use this recipe as a basic starting point, and build from there.

## TOOLS AND EQUIPMENT

can opener

medium mixing bowl

2 forks

## INGREDIENTS

1 (7-ounce) can tuna, drained

½ teaspoon salt

¼ teaspoon freshly ground pepper

½ cup mayonnaise

**Make the tuna salad:** In a medium mixing bowl, using a fork, flake the tuna. Season with the salt and pepper. Add the mayonnaise and toss lightly using 2 forks.

*Jazz It Up: Add ½ cup diced celery, 1 tablespoon minced onion, and 2 tablespoons apple cider vinegar to the usual ingredients and combine. This will increase the yield to 6 servings.*

*Pro Tip: One cup of plain yogurt with a teaspoon of mustard makes for an acceptable alternative to mayonnaise with fewer calories and less fat.*

*Store It: Refrigerate any leftover Tuna Salad in airtight containers. It will last for up to 3 days in the refrigerator.*

PER SERVING: CALORIES: 238; TOTAL FAT: 20G; SODIUM: 496MG; CHOLESTEROL: 25MG; TOTAL CARBS: 0G; FIBER: 0G; SUGAR: 0G; PROTEIN: 13G

# Macaroni Salad

**SERVES** 6

**PREP TIME:** 15 minutes

Macaroni Salad is the star side dish of family get-togethers, barbecues, and other gatherings. It has a pop of color and a bit of a crunch. You can add a lettuce leaf to the plate, and spoon the finished macaroni salad on top of the leaf for a lovely presentation.

## TOOLS AND EQUIPMENT

large mixing bowl

fork

## INGREDIENTS

5 cups cooked elbow macaroni, chilled

1 (4-ounce) jar pimientos, chopped

1 cup diced celery

¾ cup mayonnaise

1 tablespoon minced onion

1 tablespoon minced green bell pepper

1 tablespoon freshly squeezed lemon juice

1½ teaspoons salt

¼ teaspoon paprika

**Make the salad:** In a large mixing bowl, combine the macaroni, pimientos, celery, mayonnaise, onion, bell pepper, lemon juice, salt, and paprika. Toss lightly with a fork until blended.

*Jazz It Up:* Add ¼ cup cooked peas and ¼ cup chopped, cooked carrots for an added burst of flavor and color.

*Pro Tip:* Cook the macaroni al dente for best results.

PER SERVING: CALORIES: 394; TOTAL FAT: 21G; SODIUM: 779MG; CHOLESTEROL: 10MG; TOTAL CARBS: 43G; FIBER: 4G; SUGAR: 5G; PROTEIN: 8G

# Fruity Broccoli Salad

**SERVES** 4

**PREP TIME:** 10 minutes

This Fruity Broccoli Salad is a delicious way to enjoy broccoli. It has a sweetness that pairs well with the crunch of the broccoli, and the vinegar and bacon give it a savory offset. It's easy to prepare and has always been a hit with my children, even when they were younger.

## TOOLS AND EQUIPMENT

can opener

medium mixing bowl

wooden spoon

small mixing bowl

## INGREDIENTS

2 broccoli heads, broken into florets

½ cup dried cranberries

1 small red onion, chopped

½ cup mandarin orange slices, drained

½ cup plain yogurt

¼ cup sugar

1 tablespoon vinegar

12 slices of Easy Crispy Oven Bacon (page 28) or cooked bacon, crumbled

1. **Make the salad:** In a medium mixing bowl, combine the broccoli, dried cranberries, onion, and mandarin oranges.

2. **Make the dressing:** In a small mixing bowl, combine the yogurt, sugar, and vinegar. Stir until smooth. Pour the dressing over the salad, and stir until the broccoli is well coated. Sprinkle the bacon over the salad, and serve.

*Pro Tip: Make this the night before, and store in an airtight container in the refrigerator.*

PER SERVING: CALORIES: 493; TOTAL FAT: 25G; SODIUM: 1403MG; CHOLESTEROL: 65MG; TOTAL CARBS: 41G; FIBER: 6G; SUGAR: 29G; PROTEIN: 28G

# Chicken Taco Salad

**SERVES** 1

**PREP TIME:** 10 minutes / **COOK TIME:** 10 minutes

This chicken taco salad is one of my favorite go-to meals when I am home alone. It features a seasoned chicken breast, cut or shredded over a salad that is full of color and texture. It's easy to prepare and keeps hunger away.

**TOOLS AND EQUIPMENT**

large skillet

turner spatula

cooking thermometer

stirring spoon

small mixing bowl

whisk

**INGREDIENTS**

1 boneless skinless chicken breast

1 tablespoon taco seasoning

1 tablespoon butter

¼ cup corn kernels

⅓ cup ranch dressing

⅛ cup salsa

1½ tablespoons minced fresh cilantro

1 cup green leaf lettuce, shredded

1 Roma tomato, diced

¼ cup grated pepper jack cheese

1 avocado, peeled, pitted, and diced

1. **Prepare the chicken:** Season the chicken with taco seasoning. In a large skillet, melt the butter over medium-high heat. Add the chicken, and cook for 4 minutes on each side, or until the internal temperature reaches 165°F. Remove the chicken from the skillet. Add the corn to the skillet, reduce the heat to medium, and cook, stirring frequently, for 2 minutes, or until starting to brown. Remove from the heat.

2. **Make the dressing:** In a small mixing bowl, whisk together the ranch dressing, salsa, and minced cilantro.

3. **Make the salad:** Dice the chicken. In a serving bowl, layer the lettuce, chicken, tomato, cheese, corn, and avocado. Drizzle the dressing over the salad. Enjoy.

*Pro Tip: Make the dressing ahead of time to give the flavors a chance to meld.*

PER SERVING: CALORIES: 790; TOTAL FAT: 50G; SODIUM: 2252MG; CHOLESTEROL: 121MG; TOTAL CARBS: 52G; FIBER: 16G; SUGAR: 14G; PROTEIN: 42G

# Beef Taco Layer Salad

**NUT-FREE**

**SERVES** 8

**PREP TIME:** 30 minutes / **COOK TIME:** 30 minutes

This Beef Taco Layer Salad works as a taco salad, or you can set it out with chips and serve it as an appetizer. You can even use it as part of your taco bar, setting it out with flour tortillas for guests to fill with the layers and enjoy.

## TOOLS AND EQUIPMENT

can opener
box grater
medium skillet
medium mixing bowl
electric mixer
9-by-13-inch baking pan

## INGREDIENTS

1½ pounds ground chuck

1 package taco seasoning

1 (8-ounce) container sour cream

1 (8-ounce) package cream cheese

1 cup salsa

½ head iceberg lettuce, shredded

1 large yellow onion, chopped

1 (4-ounce) can pickled jalapeños (optional)

1 pound mild Cheddar cheese, shredded

2 ripe tomatoes, chopped

1. **Prepare the meat:** In a medium skillet, cook the beef over medium heat for about 7 minutes, or until browned. Drain the beef, and safely discard the grease. Mix the taco seasoning according to the package directions, and stir into the beef. Simmer for 15 to 20 minutes, or until the liquid evaporates and the mixture thickens. Remove from the heat. Let cool to room temperature.

2. **Prepare the sauce:** In a medium mixing bowl, using an electric mixer, combine the sour cream, cream cheese, and salsa until smooth.

3. **Layer the salad:** Layer all of the ingredients in a 9-by-13-inch baking pan, and garnish with chips.

*Another Idea: You can make your own taco seasoning. In a sandwich-size resealable bag, combine 3 tablespoons chili powder, 2 tablespoons paprika, 1½ tablespoons onion powder, 1 tablespoon ground cumin, and ½ tablespoon garlic powder. Mix until well combined. Use 5 tablespoons of the mixture instead of one prepackaged packet of taco seasoning.*

PER SERVING: CALORIES: 725; TOTAL FAT: 54G; SODIUM: 953MG; CHOLESTEROL: 163MG; TOTAL CARBS: 26G; FIBER: 4G; SUGAR: 4G; PROTEIN: 35G

# Cobb Salad

EXTRA QUICK, NUT-FREE

**SERVES** 4
**PREP TIME:** 15 minutes / **COOK TIME:** 10 minutes

To me, this salad's name is an acronym. Just remember "EAT COBB." It stands for Egg, Avocado, Tomato, Chicken, Onion, Bacon, and Blue Cheese. It all comes together with a bright vinaigrette dressing. This salad requires a bit of prep, but it's nothing you can't handle.

## TOOLS AND EQUIPMENT

zip-top freezer bags

rolling pin

medium skillet

cooking thermometer

jar with lid

## INGREDIENTS

## FOR THE SALAD

1 pound boneless skinless
  chicken breasts

2 tablespoons olive oil

½ teaspoon paprika

Salt

Freshly ground
  black pepper

## TO MAKE THE SALAD

1. **Cook the chicken:** One at a time, place a chicken breast in a freezer bag, squeeze the air out of it, and seal it shut (this will prevent any mess you may get from rolling it). Using a rolling pin, flatten the chicken in the bag to ½-inch thickness. Do this with each piece of chicken until all are flattened. This will help each piece to cook evenly. In a medium skillet, heat the oil over medium heat. Remove the chicken from the bags and season with the paprika and salt and pepper. Add to the skillet, and cook for 5 minutes per side, or until the internal temperature reaches 165°F. Remove from the heat. Transfer the chicken to a cutting board and let cool. Once cool enough to handle, dice.

2. **Layer the salad:** In a large bowl, assemble the salad in layers. Begin with the lettuce, then add the bacon, chicken, tomatoes, and onion, followed by the avocado and eggs, and finally sprinkle with the blue cheese.

8 cups romaine lettuce, cut into ½-inch strips

4 slices of Easy Crispy Oven Bacon (page 28) or cooked bacon, crumbled

1 cup cherry tomatoes, halved

1 cup diced yellow onion

1 avocado, peeled, pitted, and cut into small pieces or thinly sliced

4 Hardboiled Eggs (page 48)

2 ounces blue cheese, crumbled

## FOR THE VINAIGRETTE DRESSING

½ cup olive oil

¼ cup red-wine vinegar

1 tablespoon Dijon mustard

½ teaspoon salt

¼ teaspoon freshly ground black pepper

### TO MAKE THE VINAIGRETTE DRESSING

**Make the dressing:** In a jar with a lid, combine the oil, vinegar, mustard, salt, and pepper. Secure the lid and shake the jar until combined and the salt has dissolved. Drizzle the dressing over the salad.

*Pro Tip:* *You can make this salad ahead of time, cover it, and put in the refrigerator for up to 2 hours. Add the dressing when ready to serve.*

PER SERVING: CALORIES: 686; TOTAL FAT: 56G; SODIUM: 1061MG; CHOLESTEROL: 97MG; TOTAL CARBS: 13G; FIBER: 5G; SUGAR: 4G; PROTEIN: 38G

# Chapter 6

# SOLO MEALS

This chapter will give you ideas for preparing meals for yourself, or, in some cases, two people. There are soups and sandwiches, French Bread Pizza (page 96), and Avocado Toast with Egg (page 94). It's your favorite foods created on a smaller scale, so you don't have to sacrifice options when you're dining alone.

# Quesadilla

**SERVES** 1

**PREP TIME:** 5 minutes / **COOK TIME:** 5 minutes

The quesadilla is a quick meal that takes only 10 minutes to make. This is a basic recipe—cheese and tortilla, just like the original back in the 1500s. Add your own ingredients, such as fresh vegetables, beans, shredded meat, and more to customize to your own taste.

**TOOLS AND EQUIPMENT**

medium skillet

turner spatula

pastry brush

**INGREDIENTS**

1 (8-inch) flour tortilla

½ cup shredded
  Cheddar cheese

1 teaspoon oil

1. **Make the quesadilla:** In a medium skillet, cook the tortilla over medium heat for 30 seconds. Flip, and sprinkle the cheese on top. Fold the tortilla in half, brush lightly with the oil, and flip. Cook for 1 to 2 minutes, or until golden brown. Brush the top with oil and flip again, cooking for 1 to 2 minutes, or until the other side is golden brown. Remove from the heat.

2. **Serve:** Transfer the quesadilla to a cutting board and let rest for 2 minutes. Cut in half. Serve with your choice of toppings.

*Pro Tip:* Don't turn the heat up too high. Try lowering the heat a bit, and take a little more time to cook so that the quesadilla gets a crisp, golden shell.

*Store It:* These quesadillas are best right out of the pan; however, you can make them ahead of time and keep them covered in the refrigerator for up to 3 days. Reheat in the microwave for 30 seconds.

PER SERVING: CALORIES: 411; TOTAL FAT: 27G; SODIUM: 643MG; CHOLESTEROL: 59MG; TOTAL CARBS: 24G; FIBER: 1G; SUGAR: 1G; PROTEIN: 18G

# Grilled Cheese Sandwich

EXTRA QUICK, NUT-FREE, VEGETARIAN

**SERVES** 2

**PREP TIME:** 5 minutes / **COOK TIME:** 20 minutes

Grilled cheese is a delicious sandwich. It's easy to make and pairs superbly with Almost Homemade Tomato Soup (page 72). I prefer white bread and Cheddar cheese for my grilled cheese sandwiches, but you can use any type of bread and your favorite cheese: Cheddar, Swiss, mozzarella, pepper jack, or a combination of cheeses. It's up to you.

## TOOLS AND EQUIPMENT

butter knife

medium skillet

turner spatula

## INGREDIENTS

3 tablespoons butter

4 slices bread

2 slices Cheddar cheese

**Make the sandwiches:** Generously butter one side of each slice of bread. Heat a medium skillet over medium heat. Place one slice of buttered bread in the skillet, butter-side down. Top with 1 slice cheese. Place a second slice of bread on top of the cheese, butter-side up. Cook for about 4 minutes, or until the sandwich is light golden brown. Using a turner spatula, flip the sandwich over. Cook for 4 minutes, or until the other side is light golden brown and the cheese has melted. Repeat with the next sandwich.

*Jazz It Up: Make Waffle Iron Grilled Cheese. Butter one side of each slice of bread, place on a waffle grill, and top with 1 slice cheese and the second slice of bread, butter-side up. Close the waffle iron (don't smash it all the way down, let the bread begin to soften, then close it gently). Cook for 2 minutes. Press the waffle iron closed, and brown for another 2 minutes. Remove from the waffle iron. Repeat with second sandwich.*

PER SERVING: CALORIES: 404; TOTAL FAT: 28G; SODIUM: 561MG; CHOLESTEROL: 75MG; TOTAL CARBS: 24G; FIBER: 4G; SUGAR: 3G; PROTEIN: 14G

# Avocado Toast with Egg

EXTRA QUICK, NUT-FREE, VEGETARIAN

**SERVES** 1

**PREP TIME:** 5 minutes / **COOK TIME:** 10 minutes

This meal is a great balance of protein, healthy fats, and carbs. Avocado toast seems to be trending, and with good reason: It's not just easy, it's delicious. Whole-grain bread is a better choice than white sandwich bread because it offers fiber, vitamins, and minerals. You can, of course, choose the bread you prefer, including a gluten-free bread if you have an intolerance.

**TOOLS AND EQUIPMENT**

medium skillet

turner spatula

medium mixing bowl

fork

toaster

**INGREDIENTS**

1 teaspoon butter

1 large egg

1 ripe avocado, pitted and peeled

½ teaspoon freshly squeezed lemon juice

¼ teaspoon salt

⅛ teaspoon freshly ground pepper

1 slice bread

1. **Make the egg:** In a medium skillet, melt the butter over medium heat. Crack the egg into the skillet, and cook for about 2 minutes, or until the egg white turns opaque. Using a turner spatula, flip the egg, and cook for 2 to 5 minutes, or until the yolk is done to your liking. Remove from the heat.

2. **Make the avocado:** In a medium mixing bowl, use a fork to mash the avocado. Stir in the lemon juice, salt, and pepper.

3. **Make the toast:** Toast the bread in a toaster to your desired crispiness. Spread the avocado on the toast, and top with the egg.

*Jazz It Up:* Try scrambling the egg for a different texture.

*Pro Tip:* Leave some chunks when mashing your avocado. Doing so adds texture and helps hold the egg yolk when you break it.

PER SERVING: CALORIES: 465; TOTAL FAT: 36G; SODIUM: 825MG; CHOLESTEROL: 196MG; TOTAL CARBS: 27G; FIBER: 14G; SUGAR: 3G; PROTEIN: 13G

# Turkey Wrap

**SERVES** 2
**PREP TIME:** 10 minutes

These turkey wraps are stuffed with delicious turkey, carrots, cream cheese, lettuce, and cheese. They are a power snack to keep you going or an easy lunch or dinner. The wraps can be rolled and cut into attractive spirals, or you can simply roll them and let the filling be the star.

## TOOLS AND EQUIPMENT

rubber spatula

## INGREDIENTS

4 tablespoons cream cheese with chives, softened

2 (10-inch) whole-wheat tortillas

4 ounces thinly sliced deli turkey

½ cup shredded carrots

¼ cup sprouts

¼ cup cherry tomatoes, halved

2 romaine lettuce leaves, shredded

¼ cup shredded Cheddar cheese

1. **Prepare the tortillas:** Using a rubber spatula, leaving a 1-inch border without any cream cheese around the outer edge, spread 2 tablespoons of cream cheese on one side of each tortilla.

2. **Layer the wraps:** Top the cream cheese with the turkey, followed by the carrots, sprouts, tomatoes, lettuce, and cheese.

3. **Roll the wraps:** Beginning on one end of a tortilla, roll the edge toward the center. Continue rolling until you reach the other side. Repeat with the other tortilla.

*Pro Tip:* When you finish rolling the tortilla, wrap with plastic wrap and chill in refrigerator for 30 minutes. This will help set the roll and make it easier to eat.

PER SERVING: CALORIES: 506; TOTAL FAT: 26G; SODIUM: 1515MG; CHOLESTEROL: 86MG; TOTAL CARBS: 46G; FIBER: 3G; SUGAR: 6G; PROTEIN: 22G

# French Bread Pizza

EXTRA QUICK, NUT-FREE

**SERVES** 2

**PREP TIME:** 5 minutes / **COOK TIME:** 15 minutes

This is my kids' go-to for a snack and a favorite late-night adventure whenever they are hosting a sleepover. This recipe is a foundation: You can jazz it up with fresh vegetables, sausage, or any of your favorite pizza toppings.

## TOOLS AND EQUIPMENT

baking sheet

serrated knife

rubber spatula

oven mitts

## INGREDIENTS

1 loaf French bread

1 (14-ounce) jar pizza sauce

1 cup shredded mozzarella cheese

1 (6-ounce) bag pepperoni slices

1. **Prepare the bread:** Preheat the oven to 400°F. Line a baking sheet with aluminum foil. Using a serrated knife and ensuring it is parallel to the cutting board, slice the bread so you end up with a top half and a bottom half. Place cut-sides up on the baking sheet.

2. **Make the pizza:** Spread the pizza sauce onto the bread. Sprinkle with the cheese, then top with the pepperoni.

3. **Bake:** Place the baking sheet on the middle rack of the oven. Bake for 12 minutes, or until the cheese has melted. Remove from the oven.

*Jazz It Up: Add any of your favorite pizza toppings for a personalized French bread pizza.*

PER SERVING: CALORIES: 1231; TOTAL FAT: 45G; SODIUM: 3724MG; CHOLESTEROL: 97MG; TOTAL CARBS: 151G; FIBER: 9G; SUGAR: 12G; PROTEIN: 53G

# Microwave Macaroni and Cheese

**SERVES** 1
**PREP TIME:** 5 minutes / **COOK TIME:** 5 minutes

This macaroni and cheese recipe is better than the stuff in the blue box, and it makes just enough for one serving. It's a complete meal, made in the microwave. And it's creamy and cheesy, just like macaroni and cheese is supposed to be.

## TOOLS AND EQUIPMENT

2 large microwave-
  safe bowls

colander

whisk

stirring spoon

## INGREDIENTS

¾ cup cold water

⅓ cup elbow macaroni

¼ teaspoon cornstarch

4 tablespoons milk, divided

¼ cup grated
  Cheddar cheese

½ teaspoon salt

¼ teaspoon freshly
  ground pepper

1. **Make the macaroni:** In a large microwave-safe bowl, combine the water and macaroni. Microwave on high for 4 minutes. Drain.

2. **Make the sauce:** Place the cornstarch in a separate large microwave-safe bowl, then whisk in 1 tablespoon of milk until smooth. Slowly whisk in the remaining 3 tablespoons of milk. Add the cheese, salt, pepper, and cooked macaroni. Stir. Microwave on high for 1 minute.

*Pro Tip: Cooking time may vary depending on the depth and width of your bowl. Do not leave it unattended in the microwave.*

*Jazz It Up: Add a splash of hot sauce for a little kick.*

PER SERVING: CALORIES: 252; TOTAL FAT: 11G; SODIUM: 1369MG; CHOLESTEROL: 35MG; TOTAL CARBS: 25G; FIBER: 1G; SUGAR: 4G; PROTEIN: 13G

# Microwave Egg Fried Rice

DAIRY-FREE, EXTRA QUICK, NUT-FREE, VEGETARIAN

**SERVES** 1

**PREP TIME:** 5 minutes / **COOK TIME:** 3 minutes

It doesn't get much easier than this no-fuss meal, made with rice, egg, vegetables, and soy sauce. It all comes together to make a delicious egg fried rice that can work as a solo meal or as a side dish. The best part? You can do it all in the microwave.

## TOOLS AND EQUIPMENT

microwave-safe mug

small mixing bowl

whisk

fork

## INGREDIENTS

1 cup cooked jasmine rice

2 tablespoons frozen peas and carrots

1 scallion, root trimmed and green and white parts sliced

2 tablespoons shredded purple cabbage (optional)

1 large egg

1 tablespoon low-sodium soy sauce

½ teaspoon onion powder

1. **Prepare the vegetables and rice:** Put the rice in a large mug. Layer with the peas and carrots, scallion, and purple cabbage (if using). Cover the mug with plastic wrap. Using the tip of a knife, puncture in the middle. Microwave on high for 1 minute 15 seconds.

2. **Add the egg and seasoning:** In a small mixing bowl, whisk together the egg, soy sauce, and onion powder. Carefully pull back the plastic wrap, add the egg mixture, and stir. Cover the bowl again with the plastic wrap.

3. **Finish and serve:** Microwave on high for 1 minute 30 seconds. Carefully remove the plastic wrap and stir. Let rest for 1 minute. Fluff with a fork, and enjoy.

*Jazz It Up:* **Try adding leftover cooked ham, pork, or chicken.**

PER SERVING: CALORIES: 337; TOTAL FAT: 6G; SODIUM: 967MG; CHOLESTEROL: 186MG; TOTAL CARBS: 59G; FIBER: 2G; SUGAR: 3G; PROTEIN: 13G

# Vegetarian Burrito Bowl

**SERVES** 1

**PREP TIME:** 5 minutes / **COOK TIME:** 1 minute

This burrito bowl has so many possibilities. Use this recipe as a foundation, and feel free to add fresh or sautéed vegetables, such as corn, peppers, or jalapeños. Or, give the bowl some additional texture with pinto beans or chickpeas, chopped lettuce, or sliced black olives. Drizzle with enchilada or verde sauce. Top with guacamole, sliced avocado, or diced tomatoes. This is a meal ready for you to customize.

## TOOLS AND EQUIPMENT

can opener

medium microwave-
    safe bowl

## INGREDIENTS

1 cup precooked
    brown rice

½ cup black beans, drained
    and rinsed

2 tablespoons salsa

2 tablespoons shredded
    Cheddar cheese

1 tablespoon Greek yogurt

**Make the burrito bowl:** Put the brown rice in a medium microwave-safe bowl. Add the black beans, salsa, cheese, and yogurt. Microwave on high for 30 seconds. Stir, then microwave on high for another 30 seconds, or until heated through. Top with your favorite toppings.

*Pro Tip: Many grocery stores carry precooked brown rice pouches that you can boil—these are a great option for this recipe.*

PER SERVING: CALORIES: 329; TOTAL FAT: 6G; SODIUM: 281MG; CHOLESTEROL: 15MG; TOTAL CARBS: 55G; FIBER: 9G; SUGAR: 1G; PROTEIN: 15G

# Broccoli Noodle Casserole

**MAKES** 1 (8-by-8-inch) casserole
**PREP TIME:** 10 minutes / **COOK TIME:** 40 minutes

This casserole is made in the microwave. It has a crunchy crispy fried onion topping and a creamy sauce that coats the spaghetti. This recipe makes one hardy serving, or try as a side dish for two, paired with a protein.

## TOOLS AND EQUIPMENT

can opener

8-by-8-inch microwave-safe dish

colander

stirring spoon

## INGREDIENTS

4 cups water

4 ounces spaghetti, broken in half

1 (10-ounce) package frozen broccoli florets

1 (10.5-ounce) can condensed cream of mushroom soup

½ cup crispy fried onions, such as French's, divided

1. **Make the pasta:** Put the water in an 8-by-8-inch microwave-safe dish. Microwave on high for 15 minutes, or until the water reaches a rapid boil. Add the spaghetti to the boiling water. Microwave for 10 minutes on high, or until tender. Drain.

2. **Make the sauce:** Cook the broccoli in the microwave according to package directions. Add to the spaghetti. Stir in the soup and ¼ cup of crispy fried onions. Toss. Top with the remaining ¼ cup of crispy fried onions, cover with a paper towel, and microwave on high for 15 minutes. Let rest in the microwave for 2 minutes.

*Pro Tip: To save time, try cooking the spaghetti on the stovetop according to the package directions at the same time you are cooking the broccoli florets.*

*Jazz It Up: Add ½ cup grated Cheddar cheese along with the cream of mushroom soup for a cheesy broccoli noodle casserole.*

PER SERVING (2): CALORIES: 560; TOTAL FAT: 23G; SODIUM: 1146MG; CHOLESTEROL: 0MG; TOTAL CARBS: 71G; FIBER: 10G; SUGAR: 7G; PROTEIN: 14G

# Penne with Bacon and Zucchini

EXTRA QUICK, NUT-FREE

**SERVES** 1

**PREP TIME:** 15 minutes / **COOK TIME:** 15 minutes

This dish is easy to make and is great for one person. It is made with simple, fresh ingredients and comes together quickly. The creamy sauce coats the penne, and the zucchini gives this dish a pop of color. For a complete meal, this dish pairs well with a piece of garlic bread and a side salad.

## TOOLS AND EQUIPMENT

medium saucepan

colander

large skillet with lid

stirring spoon

## INGREDIENTS

4 ounces penne

1 tablespoon olive oil

½ onion, diced

3 slices of bacon, diced

1 large zucchini, diced

1 cube chicken bouillon

¼ cup water

½ cup heavy cream

1 tablespoon grated Parmesan cheese, for topping

1. **Make the penne:** Cook the penne according to the package directions. Drain.

2. **Make the sauce:** In a large skillet, heat the oil over medium heat. Add the onion and bacon. Cook for about 5 minutes, or until the onion is translucent. Add the zucchini and chicken bouillon. Cook, stirring frequently, for 3 minutes, or until the zucchini is lightly sautéed. Add the water, and stir. Cover, and cook for 6 minutes, or until the zucchini is soft and the liquid has been absorbed. Uncover, and stir in the cream. Remove from the heat.

3. **Serve:** Add the penne to the sauce, and stir. Top with the cheese, and enjoy.

*Jazz It Up:* Add 2 tablespoons chopped sun-dried tomatoes or halved cherry tomatoes to the pan with the zucchini.

PER SERVING: CALORIES: 1344; TOTAL FAT: 86G; SODIUM: 2205MG; CHOLESTEROL: 231MG; TOTAL CARBS: 101G; FIBER: 7G; SUGAR: 9G; PROTEIN: 45G

# Chili Cheese Baked Potato

**SERVES** 1

**PREP TIME:** 5 minutes / **COOK TIME:** 15 minutes

One of my family's favorite things is a baked potato bar. While this recipe isn't a full baked potato bar, it does create a delicious chili cheese baked potato that really fills you up. The best part is, with a microwave, this meal is ready in minutes.

**TOOLS AND EQUIPMENT**

fork

microwave-safe plate

paring knife

**INGREDIENTS**

1 large russet potato, pricked all over with a fork

½ tablespoon olive oil

Salt

Freshly ground black pepper

¼ tablespoon butter

¼ cup shredded Cheddar cheese

1 (15-ounce) can prepared chili

Sour cream, for topping (optional)

1. **Prepare the potato:** Rub the potato with the oil. Season with salt. Put on a microwave-safe plate. Microwave on high for 5 minutes. Turn the potato over and microwave for another 5 minutes, or until the potato is soft. Cut a slit lengthwise in the potato. Place one hand on each end of the potato and push until the center opens up. Season with salt and pepper. Using a fork, scrape and mash the inside of the potato.

2. **Make the potato:** Add the butter, cheese, and chili. Microwave for 1 minute. Top with sour cream (if using), and enjoy.

*Pro Tip: Let the potato rest in the microwave for 2 minutes before turning it over, and another 2 minutes before removing it from the microwave. This will help soften it.*

PER SERVING: CALORIES: 961; TOTAL FAT: 43G; SODIUM: 2562MG; CHOLESTEROL: 109MG; TOTAL CARBS: 117G; FIBER: 23G; SUGAR: 7G; PROTEIN: 39G

# Black Bean Burgers

**MAKES** 6 patties
**PREP TIME:** 5 minutes / **COOK TIME:** 20 minutes

This is the first recipe my son, Zac, made when he decided to follow a vegan diet. Black beans are the primary ingredient and are both very tasty and very good for us. Make these ahead of time and store the extra patties in a sealed container in the refrigerator for three to five days for quick grab-and-go meals during the week.

## TOOLS AND EQUIPMENT

can opener
colander
medium skillet
large mixing bowl
wooden spoon
medium mixing bowl

## INGREDIENTS

4 tablespoons olive
  oil, divided

½ onion, diced

1 (15.5-ounce) can black
  beans, drained and rinsed

2 slices bread, pulled
  into pieces

1 teaspoon garlic powder

1 teaspoon onion powder

½ teaspoon salt

¼ teaspoon freshly
  ground pepper

½ cup flour

1. **Prepare the onions:** In a medium skillet, heat 1 tablespoon of oil over medium heat. Add the onion, and sauté for about 5 minutes, or until soft and translucent. Remove from the heat.

2. **Make the burgers:** In a large mixing bowl, using a wooden spoon, mash the beans until they are almost smooth. Add the onion, bread, garlic powder, onion powder, salt, and pepper. Add the flour a few table-spoons at a time, and mix well. The mixture will be thick. Shape into 6 (½-inch-thick) patties.

3. **Cook:** In a medium skillet, heat 1 tablespoon of oil over medium heat. Add 2 patties, and cook for 2 minutes on each side, or until heated through. Repeat in batches of 2 with the remaining patties.

*Another Idea: If you would like to grill the patties, add 1 tablespoon olive oil to the patty mixture.*

*Jazz It Up: Black Bean Burger topping ideas include chipotle mayonnaise, lettuce, tomatoes, cheese, avocado, onion, pickles, and jalapeños.*

PER SERVING: CALORIES: 202; TOTAL FAT: 10G; SODIUM: 239MG; CHOLESTEROL: 0MG; TOTAL CARBS: 24G; FIBER: 4G; SUGAR: 1G; PROTEIN: 6G

# Lemon Chicken

**SERVES** 1

**PREP TIME:** 5 minutes, plus 30 minutes to marinate / **COOK TIME:** 25 minutes

This lemon chicken is loaded with flavor. Set aside time for the chicken to marinate for at least 30 minutes, up to four hours. You can substitute Fluffy Mashed Potatoes (page 57) for the rice and pair it all with asparagus.

**TOOLS AND EQUIPMENT**

small mixing bowl

whisk

small shallow dish

cooking thermometer

baking sheet

oven mitts

**INGREDIENTS**

1 garlic clove, minced

2 tablespoons freshly squeezed lemon juice

1 tablespoon olive oil

½ teaspoon mustard

½ teaspoon Italian seasoning

¼ teaspoon salt

¼ teaspoon freshly ground black pepper

1 chicken breast

½ cup white rice, cooked (page 58)

1 tablespoon butter

1. **Marinate the chicken:** In a small mixing bowl, whisk together the garlic, lemon juice, oil, mustard, Italian seasoning, salt, and pepper. Put the chicken in a small shallow dish and pour the marinade over the chicken. Cover with plastic wrap, and let marinate in the refrigerator for 30 minutes to 4 hours.

2. **Bake the chicken:** Preheat the oven to 350°F. Remove the chicken from the marinade, and transfer to a baking sheet. Discard the marinade. Place the baking sheet on the middle rack of the oven and bake for 25 minutes, or until the internal temperature reaches 165°F. Remove from the oven. Cover with aluminum foil, and let rest for 5 minutes.

3. **Serve:** Scoop the rice onto a plate, slice the chicken, and place on top of the rice.

*Jazz It Up:* Cut a lemon into ¼-inch slices, and place on top of the chicken before baking for additional flavor and garnish.

PER SERVING: CALORIES: 491; TOTAL FAT: 30G; SODIUM: 728MG; CHOLESTEROL: 104MG; TOTAL CARBS: 29G; FIBER: 1G; SUGAR: 1G; PROTEIN: 27G

# Parmesan-Crusted Pork Chops

NUT-FREE

**SERVES** 1

**PREP TIME:** 10 minutes / **COOK TIME:** 30 minutes

This recipe creates a tender pork chop with a slightly crisp crust of Parmesan cheese. It is delicious when paired with Fluffy Mashed Potatoes (page 57) and Green Beans with Bacon, Onion, and Garlic (page 62) or a side salad.

## TOOLS AND EQUIPMENT

8-by-8-inch baking pan

medium mixing bowl

whisk

plate

cooking thermometer

oven mitts

## INGREDIENTS

Nonstick cooking spray, for greasing

1 large egg

¼ cup grated Parmesan cheese

1 tablespoon bread crumbs

1 teaspoon paprika

1 boneless pork chop, trimmed of fat

1. **Prepare the pork chop:** Preheat the oven to 350°F. Lightly coat the bottom of an 8-by-8-inch baking pan with nonstick cooking spray. In a medium mixing bowl, whisk the egg. On a plate, combine the cheese, bread crumbs, and paprika. Stir until mixed well. Dip the pork chop in the egg to completely coat, then press each side into the Parmesan mixture. Transfer to the baking pan.

2. **Bake:** Place the baking pan on the middle rack of the oven, and bake for 30 minutes, or until the internal temperature reaches 145°F. Remove from the oven.

*Pro Tip: Place a wire rack in the baking pan, and place the pork chop on top of it for a crispier crust.*

*Another Idea: Panko bread crumbs offer the best texture in this recipe, but any type of bread crumbs will work.*

*Jazz It Up: Serve on top of spaghetti with marinara sauce.*

PER SERVING: CALORIES: 419; TOTAL FAT: 25G; SODIUM: 820MG; CHOLESTEROL: 261MG; TOTAL CARBS: 8G; FIBER: 1G; SUGAR: 1G; PROTEIN: 42G

# Ham and Chicken Casserole

**SERVES** 2

**PREP TIME:** 10 minutes / **COOK TIME:** 30 minutes

This casserole features both chicken and ham in a creamy sauce over egg noodles. It works great with leftovers.

## TOOLS AND EQUIPMENT

8-by-8-inch baking pan

2 medium saucepans

colander

stirring spoon

whisk

oven mitts

## INGREDIENTS

Nonstick cooking spray

4 ounces egg noodles

2 tablespoons butter

2 tablespoons
  all-purpose flour

1 cup milk

½ cup diced
  cooked chicken

½ cup diced cooked ham

¼ cup chopped celery

1 teaspoon paprika

¼ teaspoon salt

¼ teaspoon freshly
  ground pepper

½ cup shredded
  Cheddar cheese

1. **Make the noodles:** Preheat the oven to 400°F. Lightly coat the interior of an 8-by-8-inch baking pan with non-stick cooking spray. Cook the egg noodles according to the package directions. Drain.

2. **Make the sauce:** In a medium saucepan, melt the butter over medium-low heat. Stir in the flour, and cook for about 3 minutes, or until starting to bubble. Slowly whisk in the milk. Stirring constantly, cook until thick and smooth. Remove from the heat.

3. **Make the casserole:** Add the noodles to the sauce. Add the chicken, ham, celery, paprika, salt, and pepper. Toss to coat the noodles. Spoon into the baking pan. Transfer to the oven, and bake for 15 minutes. Remove from the oven. Top with the cheese, return to the oven, and bake for 5 minutes, or until the cheese has melted. Remove from the oven.

*Jazz It Up:* Try adding ¼ cup leftover green beans, corn, or peas to the mixture in step 3.

*Pro Tip:* Let the casserole rest for 5 minutes before serving.

PER SERVING: CALORIES: 531; TOTAL FAT: 29G; SODIUM: 1084MG; CHOLESTEROL: 140MG; TOTAL CARBS: 35G; FIBER: 2G; SUGAR: 7G; PROTEIN: 32G

# Beef Stroganoff

**SERVES** 3

**PREP TIME:** 10 minutes / **COOK TIME:** 20 minutes

This beef stroganoff recipe combines tender chunks of beef with mushrooms in a rich, beefy gravy mixed with sour cream, served over egg noodles.

## TOOLS AND EQUIPMENT

large skillet

resealable bag

tongs

medium pot

colander

plate

stirring spoon

## INGREDIENTS

3 tablespoons butter, divided

2 tablespoons flour

¼ teaspoon salt

⅛ teaspoon black pepper

8 ounces beef sirloin steak

½ cup beef broth

8 ounces wide egg noodles

1 cup chopped onions

1 garlic clove, minced

½ cup sliced mushrooms

1 teaspoon Worcestershire sauce

¼ cup sour cream

1. **Prepare the beef:** Thinly slice the steak. Place the flour, salt, and pepper into a resealable bag. Add the steak, seal the bag, and shake to coat. In a large skillet, melt 1 tablespoon of butter over medium heat. Add the steak to the skillet, and cook for about 3 minutes per side, or until browned. Remove the steak from the pan. Add the broth.

2. **Cook the noodles:** Cook the noodles according to the package directions. Drain. Transfer to a plate, and toss with 1 tablespoon of butter.

3. **Prepare the vegetables:** Melt the remaining 1 tablespoon of butter in the skillet used to cook the steak. Add the onions, and cook for about 5 minutes or until translucent. Add the garlic and mushrooms. Cook, stirring occasionally, for 5 minutes, or until the mushrooms have softened.

4. **Finish the sauce:** Add the Worcestershire sauce, then stir in the sour cream. Remove from the heat. Spoon over the noodles, and enjoy.

PER SERVING: CALORIES: 436; TOTAL FAT: 21G; SODIUM: 442MG; CHOLESTEROL: 71MG; TOTAL CARBS: 37G; FIBER: 2G; SUGAR: 3G; PROTEIN: 26G

EASIEST CHEESIEST TORTELLINI BAKE, PAGE 133

# Chapter 7

# FAMILY MEALS

Treat your family to dinner with one of the recipes from this chapter. It offers main course casseroles, seafood, pasta, and plenty of chicken options. The recipes in this chapter include Easy Lasagna (page 120), Easy Shrimp Scampi (page 114), Tater Tot Casserole (page 124), Easy Slow Cooker Chicken Parmesan (page 127), and Baked Chili Cheese Dogs (page 113).

# Aunt Bea's Chicken Wings

**MAKES** 30 wings

**PREP TIME:** 5 minutes / **COOK TIME:** 1 hour 30 minutes

This recipe comes from my husband's Aunt Bea, and it's a favorite, not just for how good the wings are, but also for how easy they are to make. Just four ingredients make them easy to create for a snack, appetizer, or game-day party platter.

**TOOLS AND EQUIPMENT**

9-by-13-inch baking pan

tongs

oven mitts

**INGREDIENTS**

Nonstick cooking spray, for greasing

30 chicken wings

1 tablespoon lemon pepper

¾ cup cooking sherry

¼ cup soy sauce

1. **Prepare the chicken wings:** Preheat the oven to 350°F. Lightly coat the bottom of a 9-by-13-inch baking pan with nonstick cooking spray. Rinse the wings and pat dry with a paper towel. Season with the lemon pepper. Put the wings in the prepared baking pan. In a small mixing bowl, combine the sherry and soy sauce. Pour the sauce over the wings.

2. **Bake:** Place the baking pan on the middle rack of the oven. Bake for 1½ hours, turning once, or until cooked through. Remove from the oven.

*Pro Tip: Easily coat the chicken wings by putting the sauce in a resealable gallon-size bag. Add the chicken wings in small batches, seal the bag, and shake to coat the chicken. Repeat until all the wings are coated.*

PER SERVING (5 WINGS): CALORIES: 827; TOTAL FAT: 54G; SODIUM: 1385MG; CHOLESTEROL: 194MG; TOTAL CARBS: 29G; FIBER: 1G; SUGAR: 0G; PROTEIN: 50G

# Great Northern Beans

**SERVES** 6

**PREP TIME:** 10 minutes / **COOK TIME:** 20 minutes

By their nature, Great Northern beans have no cholesterol, plenty of complex carbs, and no fat. They are high in fiber and an excellent source of protein. I like them with ham and cooked in chicken broth, but meatless is also an option. If you want to make this recipe vegetarian, replace the chicken broth with water and omit the ham.

## TOOLS AND EQUIPMENT

vegetable peeler

can opener

large saucepan

stirring spoon

## INGREDIENTS

1 tablespoon butter

1 small onion, coarsely chopped

2 medium carrots, peeled and cut into rounds

2 (15.5-ounce) cans Great Northern beans, drained and rinsed

2½ cups chicken broth

2 cups diced cooked ham

1. **Prepare the onion and carrots:** In a large saucepan, melt the butter over medium heat. Add the onions and carrots and cook, stirring frequently, for 7 minutes, or until the onions are translucent and the carrots begin to soften.

2. **Cook the beans:** Add the beans, chicken broth, and ham. Cook for about 10 minutes or until heated through. Remove from the heat.

*Pro Tip: When the beans are done cooking, use a large spoon to mash some of them against the side of the pot. Repeat several times, stirring after each mashing. This will thicken your pot of beans.*

*Jazz It Up: Drain 1 can diced tomatoes, and add to the saucepan with the chicken broth.*

PER SERVING: CALORIES: 222; TOTAL FAT: 13G; SODIUM: 671MG; CHOLESTEROL: 41MG; TOTAL CARBS: 24G; FIBER: 8G; SUGAR: 2G; PROTEIN: 17G

# Sloppy Joes

**SERVES** 4

**PREP TIME:** 5 minutes / **COOK TIME:** 10 minutes

The origin of the sloppy joe sandwich is typically credited to Floyd Angell's Café cook, Joe, in Sioux City, Iowa. He is said to have added tomato sauce to his "loose meat" sandwiches, and they became popular.

**TOOLS AND EQUIPMENT**

large skillet

spoon

**INGREDIENTS**

1 pound ground beef

¾ cup ketchup

¼ cup mustard

2 tablespoons brown sugar

2 tablespoons Worcestershire sauce

4 hamburger buns

1. **Make the Sloppy Joe:** Put the beef in a large skillet, and cook over medium heat for about 5 minutes or until browned. Drain the beef, and safely discard the grease. Add the ketchup, mustard, sugar, and Worcestershire sauce. Stir until well combined. Cook for about 5 minutes or until warmed through. Remove from the heat.

2. **Serve:** Scoop equal amounts of the meat mixture onto each of the hamburger buns, and serve.

*Jazz It Up:* Add 1 small chopped onion to the beef while browning.

*Pro Tip:* Toasting the hamburger buns in the oven at 350°F for 3 minutes will help keep the bun firm as you eat.

PER SERVING: CALORIES: 395; TOTAL FAT: 13G; SODIUM: 877MG; CHOLESTEROL: 70MG; TOTAL CARBS: 42G; FIBER: 3G; SUGAR: 20G; PROTEIN: 29G

# Baked Chili Cheese Dogs

NUT-FREE

**SERVES** 8

**PREP TIME:** 5 minutes / **COOK TIME:** 40 minutes

Say bye to boiling hot dogs, and offer these delicious chili dogs to your family instead. This Baked Chili Cheese Dog is a hot dog topped with chili, cheese, mustard, and onion, then baked in the oven for a crusted bun. We use canned hot dog chili, but you can use chili with the meat and beans of your choice.

## TOOLS AND EQUIPMENT

can opener

9-by-13-inch baking pan

small mixing bowl

stirring spoon

butter knife

oven mitts

## INGREDIENTS

Nonstick cooking spray

2 tablespoons mayonnaise

2 tablespoons mustard

8 hot dog buns

8 hot dogs

1 (10-ounce) can hot
    dog chili

1 small onion, chopped

1 jalapeño pepper, seeded
    and chopped

1 cup shredded cheese

1. **Prepare the buns:** Preheat the oven to 350°F. Line a 9-by-13-inch baking pan with aluminum foil. Coat the foil with nonstick cooking spray. In a small mixing bowl, stir together the mayonnaise and mustard until well combined. Open up the hot dog buns. Using a butter knife, spread a thin layer of the mayonnaise and mustard mixture all over the inside of each bun. Put the buns in the baking pan.

2. **Make the chili dogs:** Place 1 hot dog on each bun. Cover each hot dog with 2 heaping tablespoons of hot dog chili. Top each chili dog with onion and jalapeño, then top with cheese.

3. **Bake:** Tent foil over the hot dogs so the cheese doesn't stick to it. Place on the middle rack of the oven, and bake for 40 minutes, or until the buns are golden and the chili looks firm.

*Pro Tip: Spray the foil used to cover the hot dogs with nonstick cooking spray to keep the cheese from sticking to it.*

PER SERVING: CALORIES: 388; TOTAL FAT: 24G; SODIUM: 994MG; CHOLESTEROL: 45MG; TOTAL CARBS: 29G; FIBER: 3G; SUGAR: 5G; PROTEIN: 15G

# Easy Shrimp Scampi

**SERVES** 4
**PREP TIME:** 5 minutes / **COOK TIME:** 5 minutes

Scampi are small crustaceans that look like a crayfish with longer claws. They are a delicacy in Europe. A classic Italian preparation of scampi is to sauté them in olive oil, onion, garlic, and white wine. Scampi are hard to find in the United States, so shrimp is often used as a replacement.

## TOOLS AND EQUIPMENT

large skillet

stirring spoon

## INGREDIENTS

2 tablespoons butter

2 tablespoons vegetable oil

1 pound shrimp, peeled

1 scallion, white parts only, sliced thinly

2 teaspoons minced garlic

2 teaspoons chopped fresh parsley

¼ teaspoon freshly ground black pepper

2 tablespoons freshly squeezed lemon juice

**Make the scampi:** In a large skillet, heat the butter and oil over medium heat. Add the shrimp, scallion, garlic, parsley, and pepper. Cook, stirring, for 3 to 4 minutes, or until the shrimp turn pink. Remove from the heat. Stir in the lemon juice. Serve over white rice (page 58) or noodles.

*Jazz It Up:* Serve over spinach-and-cheese ravioli.

*Pro Tip:* You can use ¼ cup butter and omit the vegetable oil. Reduce the heat to medium-low, and cook for 5 minutes. The butter will begin to brown, which creates a more complex flavor.

PER SERVING: CALORIES: 187; TOTAL FAT: 13G; SODIUM: 334MG; CHOLESTEROL: 135MG; TOTAL CARBS: 1G; FIBER: 0G; SUGAR: 0G; PROTEIN: 18G

# Mustard and Maple-Glazed Chicken

DAIRY-FREE, GLUTEN-FREE, NUT-FREE

**SERVES** 4

**PREP TIME:** 5 minutes / **COOK TIME:** 40 minutes

Chicken is a staple at my house. It can be prepared so many ways, and so many textures can be created. This recipe is easy and packed with flavor. The "gravy" is tangy and delicious drizzled over the chicken or served on white rice (page 58) or Fluffy Mashed Potatoes (page 57).

## TOOLS AND EQUIPMENT

8-by-8-inch baking pan

small mixing bowl

spoon

cooking thermometer

oven mitts

## INGREDIENTS

Nonstick cooking spray, for greasing

½ cup Dijon mustard

¼ cup maple syrup

1 tablespoon rice vinegar

4 chicken breasts

Salt

Freshly ground pepper

Chopped fresh rosemary, for garnish

1. **Make the "gravy":** Preheat the oven to 450°F. Line an 8-by-8-inch baking pan with aluminum foil. Coat the foil with nonstick cooking spray. In a small mixing bowl, mix together the mustard, maple syrup, and vinegar.

2. **Make the chicken:** Put the chicken in the baking pan. Season with salt and pepper. Pour the "gravy" over the chicken. Place the baking pan in the oven, and roast for 20 minutes. Remove from the oven. Spoon the gravy over the chicken, return to the oven, and roast for another 20 minutes, or until the internal temperature reaches 165°F. Remove from the oven. Sprinkle with fresh rosemary.

*Helpful Hint: If you don't have rice vinegar, you can use white vinegar.*

PER SERVING: CALORIES: 196; TOTAL FAT: 3G; SODIUM: 470MG; CHOLESTEROL: 65MG; TOTAL CARBS: 15G; FIBER: 1G; SUGAR: 12G; PROTEIN: 27G

# Famous Chicken

NUT-FREE

**SERVES** 4

**PREP TIME:** 15 minutes / **COOK TIME:** 45 to 55 minutes

This recipe got its name from my son, who, when he was four, asked for "Famous Chicken" for dinner. When I told him I didn't know what that was, he answered, "*That chicken that when you make it you are famous because everyone wants some.*"

## TOOLS AND EQUIPMENT

large pot

stirring spoon

tongs

whisk

cooking thermometer

## INGREDIENTS

2 tablespoons butter

4 bone-in skin-on chicken breasts

1 (8-ounce) can sliced or whole mushrooms

1 (10.5-ounce) can cream of mushroom soup

½ cup grape juice (optional)

½ cup water

1½ teaspoons paprika

¼ teaspoon salt

⅛ teaspoon freshly ground black pepper

1. **Prepare the chicken:** In a large pot, melt the butter over medium heat. Place the chicken, skin-side down, in the butter. Add the mushrooms, and cook, stirring the mushrooms, for about 7 minutes or until the chicken skin is golden brown. Using tongs, turn the chicken over and cook for about 5 minutes or until browned.

2. **Prepare the sauce:** Remove the chicken from the pot. Add the soup, grape juice (if using), water, paprika, salt, and pepper. Cook, whisking, until smooth. Bring to a slow boil.

3. **Put it all together:** Add the chicken to the sauce, reduce the heat to medium-low, and simmer for 30 to 40 minutes, or until the internal temperature of the chicken reaches 165°F.

*Jazz It Up:* Serve this dish with rice. Start your rice (page 58) once you set the timer in step 3. That way the rice will be ready at the same time as the chicken.

PER SERVING: CALORIES: 323; TOTAL FAT: 14G; SODIUM: 509MG; CHOLESTEROL: 145MG; TOTAL CARBS: 6G; FIBER: 1G; SUGAR: 2G; PROTEIN: 40G

# Linguine with Clam Sauce

**SERVES** 4

**PREP TIME:** 10 minutes / **COOK TIME:** 20 minutes

This recipe is a simple pasta dish. The parsley and basil add a pop of color. The red pepper flakes give this pasta a little heat that works perfectly with the clams.

**TOOLS AND EQUIPMENT**

can opener

large skillet

stirring spoon

large pot

colander

**INGREDIENTS**

½ cup olive oil

½ cup butter

2 garlic cloves,
  coarsely chopped

1 (8-ounce) can
  chopped clams

¼ cup fresh
  parsley, chopped

1 teaspoon dried basil

½ teaspoon red
  pepper flakes

½ teaspoon freshly ground
  black pepper

1 (16-ounce)
  package linguine

Grated Parmesan cheese,
  for topping

1. **Prepare the sauce:** In a large skillet, heat the oil and butter over medium-low heat. Add the garlic, and simmer for 2 minutes, or until fragrant and golden. Add the clams with their liquid, parsley, basil, red pepper flakes, and black pepper. Simmer for 20 minutes, or until the sauce has slightly reduced.

2. **Prepare the linguine:** Prepare the linguine according to the package directions. Drain.

3. **Bring it all together:** Add the linguine to the sauce, and mix to coat. Remove from the heat. Transfer to bowls, and top with cheese before serving.

*Pro Tip:* Save the red pepper flakes that come with pizza deliveries.

*Jazz It Up:* Add black olives to the dish just before serving.

PER SERVING: CALORIES: 902; TOTAL FAT: 52G; SODIUM: 531MG; CHOLESTEROL: 352MG; TOTAL CARBS: 87G; FIBER: 4G; SUGAR: 2G; PROTEIN: 24G

# Easy Chicken Tetrazzini

**SERVES** 4

**PREP TIME:** 10 minutes / **COOK TIME:** 25 minutes

This Chicken Tetrazzini is a white sauce-baked spaghetti with chunks of tender chicken and mushrooms.

## TOOLS AND EQUIPMENT

9-by-13-inch baking pan

small mixing bowl

whisk

medium saucepan

stirring spoon

oven mitts

## INGREDIENTS

Nonstick cooking spray

1 large egg yolk

2 tablespoons milk

6 tablespoons
  butter, divided

8 ounces
  mushrooms, sliced

1. **Prepare the egg:** Preheat the oven to 350°F. Coat the interior of a 9-by-13-inch baking pan with nonstick cooking spray. In a small mixing bowl, whisk together the egg yolk and milk.

2. **Prepare the sauce:** In a medium saucepan, melt 4 tablespoons of butter over medium heat. Add the mushrooms and bell pepper. Cook, stirring constantly, for 3 minutes, or until the mushrooms wilt and the bell pepper starts to soften. Stir in the flour, pepper, and nutmeg. Cook, stirring constantly, for 2 minutes, or until the mixture starts to thicken. Reduce the heat to low, and add the half-and-half, stirring until smooth and thickened. Add the chicken, and stir to coat. Remove from the heat. Stir in the egg yolk and milk mixture.

1 green bell pepper, cut
  into strips

3 tablespoons flour

½ teaspoon pepper

¼ teaspoon
  ground nutmeg

2½ cups half-and-half

3 cups diced
  cooked chicken

8 ounces spaghetti, cooked
  and drained

½ cup grated
  Parmesan cheese

3. **Bake:** Put the cooked spaghetti in the baking pan.
Spoon the sauce over the spaghetti. Sprinkle with
Parmesan cheese, and dot with the remaining
2 tablespoons of butter. Place on the middle rack of the
oven, and bake for 20 minutes, or until golden brown.
Remove from the oven.

*Store It:* *Store leftovers in a sealed container in the
refrigerator for up to 3 days.*

PER SERVING: CALORIES: 817; TOTAL FAT: 43G; SODIUM: 391MG;
CHOLESTEROL: 246MG; TOTAL CARBS: 55G; FIBER: 7G; SUGAR: 4G;
PROTEIN: 51G

# Easy Lasagna

**SERVES** 4

**PREP TIME:** 15 minutes / **COOK TIME:** 35 minutes

A time-saving tip for when you make lasagna is to make two at the same time. Gather all of the ingredients for two, make one and put it in the oven for dinner, then assemble a second lasagna to freeze for an easy dinner another night. It doesn't take much longer to make the second lasagna.

## TOOLS AND EQUIPMENT

large pot

colander

large skillet

rubber spatula

medium mixing bowl

stirring spoon

9-by-13-inch baking pan

spoon

oven mitts

## INGREDIENTS

½ cup chopped onion

1 pound ground beef

2 (24-ounce) jars
    marinara sauce

1. **Brown the beef:** Preheat the oven to 400°F. Put the onion and beef in a large skillet, and cook, using a rubber spatula to break up the meat, over medium-high heat for about 5 minutes, or until the beef has browned and the onion is translucent. Remove from the heat. Drain and safely discard the grease. Add the marinara sauce, and stir.

2. **Make the filling:** In a medium mixing bowl, combine the cottage cheese, ¾ cup of Parmesan cheese, and the eggs. Stir until well blended.

3. **Assemble the lasagna:** Spread 2 cups of beef sauce into a 9-by-13-inch baking pan so it covers the bottom. Layer 4 noodles over the sauce. Spoon half the cheese mixture on top of the noodles. Sprinkle 1½ cups of mozzarella on top of the cheese mixture. Then continue layering: 2 cups of beef sauce, 4 noodles, the remaining cheese mixture, and remaining 1½ cups of mozzarella. Place a final layer of noodles on top of the mozzarella, cover with the remaining beef sauce, and top with the remaining ¼ cup of Parmesan cheese.

3 cups small-curd
cottage cheese

1 cup grated Parmesan
cheese, divided

2 large eggs

12 lasagna noodles, cooked
and drained

3 cups shredded mozzarella
cheese, divided

Fresh basil leaves, torn, for
garnish (optional)

4. **Bake:** Place the baking pan on the middle rack of the
oven and bake for 30 minutes, or until the sauce has
thickened and the cheese has melted. Remove from the
oven. Let rest for 5 minutes before serving. Garnish with
fresh basil leaves (if using) for a fancier look.

*Pro Tip: The longer you rest the lasagna, the thicker the
sauce will be. Rest for up to 12 minutes before serving.*

*Store It: It's easy to double this recipe and make two
lasagnas at the same time. You can then freeze one for
dinner another night. To do this, assemble the lasagna
(do not bake), and cover tightly with aluminum foil before
freezing. When you're ready to eat, thaw the lasagna to
room temperature, and bake at 350°F for 50 minutes.*

PER SERVING: CALORIES: 1057; TOTAL FAT: 54G; SODIUM: 2718MG;
CHOLESTEROL: 288MG; TOTAL CARBS: 73G; FIBER: 3G; SUGAR: 24G;
PROTEIN: 74G

# Cheese, Chili, and Tomato Casserole

NUT-FREE

**SERVES** 8

**PREP TIME:** 15 minutes / **COOK TIME:** 50 minutes

Legend has it this casserole appeared in a 1979 cookbook of recipes collected by a ten-year-old girl named Cara Connery. She sent letters to celebrities at the time asking for their favorite recipes to help raise money for the American Cancer Society. It is said that a casserole similar to this one was sent to her from John Wayne, a popular movie actor.

## TOOLS AND EQUIPMENT

9-by-13-inch baking pan

large skillet

small mixing bowl

rubber spatula

oven mitts

## INGREDIENTS

Nonstick cooking spray, for greasing

2 pounds ground beef

2 (1-ounce) packages mild taco seasoning

⅔ cup water

1. **Prepare the beef:** Preheat the oven to 350°F. Coat the interior of a 9-by-13-inch baking pan with non-stick cooking spray. Put the beef in a large skillet, and cook over medium-high heat for about 5 minutes, or until browned. Drain the beef, and safely discard the grease. Add the taco seasoning and water. Bring to a boil. Reduce the heat to medium-low, and cook, stirring occasionally, for about 7 minutes, or until the water has reduced. Remove from the heat.

2. **Prepare the casserole:** Press the biscuits into the bottom of the baking pan (they should be flat and resemble more of a crust than biscuits when you are done). Then layer the remaining ingredients in the following order: ground beef, tomatoes, onion, bell pepper, and jalapeño. In a small mixing bowl, mix together 1½ cups of cheese, the sour cream, and mayonnaise. Spread on top of the casserole. Top with the remaining 1½ cups of cheese.

1 (16.3-ounce) can refrigerated biscuits

4 medium tomatoes, sliced

1 cup chopped onion

½ cup chopped green bell pepper

½ cup diced jalapeño peppers

3 cups shredded Cheddar cheese, divided

2 cups sour cream

1 cup mayonnaise

3. **Bake:** Place the baking pan on the middle rack of the oven and bake for 25 to 35 minutes, or until the crust is golden brown. Remove from the oven. Let rest for 5 minutes before serving.

*Jazz It Up:* **Try adding 1 cup chopped ham to the meat mixture.**

PER SERVING: CALORIES: 843; TOTAL FAT: 62G; SODIUM: 1534MG; CHOLESTEROL: 150MG; TOTAL CARBS: 33G; FIBER: 2G; SUGAR: 7G; PROTEIN: 39G

# Tater Tot Casserole

**SERVES** 8

**PREP TIME:** 10 minutes / **COOK TIME:** 35 minutes

This tater tot casserole is classic comfort food. It's packed with corn, cheese, and meat, all coated in a thick and creamy sauce. It's a meal everyone loves.

## TOOLS AND EQUIPMENT

can opener

9-by-13-inch baking pan

large skillet

large mixing bowl

stirring spoon

oven mitts

## INGREDIENTS

Nonstick cooking spray, for greasing

1¼ pounds ground beef

1 (15.25-ounce) can corn kernels

1 (10.5-ounce) can cream of mushroom soup

1 (4-ounce) can diced green chiles

½ teaspoon salt

½ teaspoon freshly ground pepper

1 (32-ounce) bag frozen tater tots

1½ cups shredded Cheddar cheese

1. **Brown the meat:** Preheat the oven to 425°F. Coat the interior of a 9-by-13-inch baking pan with nonstick cooking spray. Put the beef in a large skillet, and cook over medium heat for about 5 minutes or until browned. Remove from the heat. Drain the beef, and safely discard the grease.

2. **Make the casserole:** In a large mixing bowl, combine the corn, soup, chiles, salt, pepper, and beef and stir until well mixed. Pour into the prepared baking pan. Top with the tater tots.

3. **Bake:** Place the baking pan on the middle rack of the oven, and bake for about 30 minutes or until the casserole is bubbly and the tater tots are golden. Remove from the oven. Sprinkle the cheese evenly over the top of the casserole while still hot. Let rest for 5 minutes before serving.

*Pro Tip:* The tater tots will be crispier if you stand them on the smaller ends, rather than rest them on their sides.

PER SERVING: CALORIES: 448; TOTAL FAT: 24G; SODIUM: 953MG; CHOLESTEROL: 66MG; TOTAL CARBS: 34G; FIBER: 4G; SUGAR: 5G; PROTEIN: 23G

# Homemade Chicken Pot Pie

**SERVES** 6 to 8

**PREP TIME:** 15 minutes / **COOK TIME:** 30 minutes

This Homemade Chicken Pot Pie is the ultimate comfort food. It's food like Grandma used to make with the mixture of tender meat and vegetables in a savory sauce.

## TOOLS AND EQUIPMENT

can opener

large pot

deep-dish pie pan

fork

oven mitts

## INGREDIENTS

1 (3-pound) bag frozen precooked diced chicken breasts

2 (10-ounce) bags frozen mixed vegetables

3 (10.5-ounce) cans cream of chicken soup

1 (10.5-ounce) can cream of celery soup

2 tablespoons milk

¼ teaspoon salt

⅛ teaspoon freshly ground pepper

Nonstick cooking spray

1 box refrigerated pie crusts, at room temperature

1. **Prepare the filling:** Preheat the oven to 425°F. In a large pot, combine the chicken, vegetables, cream of chicken soup, cream of celery soup, milk, salt, and pepper. Bring to a boil over medium heat. Cook, stirring frequently, for 5 minutes, or until thickened slightly. Remove from the heat.

2. **Prepare the pie shell:** Meanwhile, coat the interior of a deep-dish pie pan with nonstick cooking spray. Unroll 1 pie crust over the pan, working it into the edge of the pan so it fits snugly.

3. **Fill the pie shell:** Pour the filling into the prepared pie crust. Unroll the second pie crust on top of the filling, and tuck the edges into the pan. (You can also crimp the edges, if you prefer.) Using a fork, poke holes in the top crust to let the pie vent during cooking.

4. **Bake:** Transfer the pie pan to the oven, and bake for 25 minutes, or until the crust is golden brown. Remove from the oven. Let cool for 5 minutes before serving.

*Pro Tip: For a thicker sauce, add 1 tablespoon cornstarch to the filling.*

PER SERVING: CALORIES: 670; TOTAL FAT: 29G; SODIUM: 1464MG; CHOLESTEROL: 144MG; TOTAL CARBS: 42G; FIBER: 4G; SUGAR: 4G; PROTEIN: 57G

# Slow Cooker Chicken Alfredo

**SERVES** 6 to 8
**PREP TIME:** 10 minutes / **COOK TIME:** 2½ to 3 hours

I wanted to include a couple of recipes to show how convenient and easy a slow cooker can be. One of the ways I learned to cook was with the slow cooker. Slow cooker recipes typically require minimal preparation and free you from standing over the stove while cooking.

**TOOLS AND EQUIPMENT**

large skillet

slow cooker

stirring spoon

**INGREDIENTS**

2 tablespoons
   unsalted butter

8 ounces
   mushrooms, sliced

2 garlic cloves, minced

1½ pounds boneless
   skinless chicken breasts,
   cut into strips or diced

Salt

Freshly ground pepper

2 (15-ounce) jars
   alfredo sauce

½ cup grated
   Parmesan cheese

1. **Prepare the mushrooms:** In a large skillet, melt the butter over medium heat. Add the mushrooms, and cook, stirring occasionally, for about 5 minutes or until tender. Transfer to a slow cooker.

2. **Make the sauce:** Add the garlic and chicken. Season with salt and pepper. Stir in the alfredo sauce. Put the lid on the slow cooker, and cook on high for 2½ to 3 hours (or on low for 5 to 6 hours), or until the internal temperature of the chicken reaches 165°F and the sauce is hot and bubbly. Turn off the slow cooker. Stir in the cheese right before serving.

*Pro Tip:* Using a slow cooker bag will make clean up easy, though it is not necessary.

PER SERVING: CALORIES: 539; TOTAL FAT: 40G; SODIUM: 959MG; CHOLESTEROL: 193MG; TOTAL CARBS: 9G; FIBER: 0G; SUGAR: 3G; PROTEIN: 40G

# Easy Slow Cooker Chicken Parmesan

**NUT-FREE**

**SERVES** 4

**PREP TIME:** 10 minutes / **COOK TIME:** 3 hours

While Chicken Parmesan may seem like it is Italian, it actually originated in the Italian-American communities of the United States. You can serve this Chicken Parmesan over noodles, such as spaghetti, or with a side salad and garlic bread.

## TOOLS AND EQUIPMENT

slow cooker

small mixing bowl

fork

large plate

## INGREDIENTS

1 tablespoon olive oil

1 large egg

½ cup seasoned Italian bread crumbs

¼ cup Parmesan cheese

¼ teaspoon salt

¼ teaspoon freshly ground black pepper

4 boneless, skinless chicken breasts

1 cup shredded mozzarella cheese

1 (15-ounce) jar marinara sauce

1. **Prepare the chicken:** Coat the bottom of a slow cooker with the oil. In a small mixing bowl, beat the egg with a fork. On a large plate, combine the bread crumbs, cheese, salt, and pepper. Dip the chicken into the egg, then dredge it in the bread crumb mixture, coating both sides. Put the chicken breasts in the slow cooker. Sprinkle ¼ cup of mozzarella cheese on each chicken breast. Pour the jar of marinara sauce over the chicken and cheese.

2. **Cook:** Put the lid on the slow cooker and cook on high for 3 hours (or on low for 5 to 6 hours), or until the internal temperature of the chicken reaches 165°F. Turn off the slow cooker.

*Store It: To store leftovers, place the chicken in an 8-by-8-inch baking pan, and top with any remaining sauce. Cover with aluminum foil, and store in the refrigerator for up to 2 days.*

PER SERVING: CALORIES: 324; TOTAL FAT: 13G; SODIUM: 1174MG; CHOLESTEROL: 137MG; TOTAL CARBS: 12G; FIBER: 2G; SUGAR: 5G; PROTEIN: 38G

# Easy Meat Loaf

NUT-FREE

**SERVES** 6 to 8

**PREP TIME:** 10 minutes / **COOK TIME:** 1½ hours

I make this meat loaf at least once a week. It is moist and delicious. The best part, however, might just be the "sticky sauce" you add at the end. It's ooey-gooey goodness that really elevates the meat loaf.

**TOOLS AND EQUIPMENT**

small mixing bowl

stirring spoon

4½-by-8½-inch loaf pan

large mixing bowl

rubber spatula

cooking thermometer

oven mitts

**INGREDIENTS**

⅔ cup ketchup

1 tablespoon plus
2 teaspoons packed
brown sugar

1 tablespoon dry mustard

2 teaspoons
Worcestershire sauce

1. **Make the sticky sauce:** In a small mixing bowl, combine the ketchup, sugar, mustard, and Worcestershire sauce. Stir until the sugar has dissolved.

2. **Make the meat loaf:** Preheat the oven to 350°F. Line a 4½-by-8½-inch loaf pan with aluminum foil. In a large mixing bowl, combine the beef, bread crumbs, cheese, eggs, garlic, steak seasoning, salt, and pepper. Mix with your clean hands until there are no large pockets of bread crumbs. Press the meat mixture into the loaf pan. Leaving about a ½-inch border on all sides, create a well running lengthwise down the center of the loaf to hold the sauce. Pour half the sauce into the well, and spread evenly.

3. **Bake:** Place the loaf pan on the middle rack of the oven, and bake for 1 to 1½ hours, or until the internal temperature reaches 160°F. Remove from the oven. Set the oven to broil, and carefully position the cooking rack as close as possible to the heating element. Being careful not to pour out the sauce, safely pour off any grease from the loaf pan. Add the remaining sauce to the top of the meat loaf, and return to the oven on the top rack. Broil for 4 minutes, or until caramelized. Keep a close eye; you do not want the sauce to burn.

2 pounds ground beef

1½ cups bread crumbs

1 cup grated
  Parmesan cheese

4 large eggs

1 garlic clove, minced

1 teaspoon steak seasoning

1 teaspoon salt

1 teaspoon freshly
  ground pepper

*Pro Tip:* *Use 2 layers of aluminum foil when you line the loaf pan and fold 2 inches of foil over the long edges of the pan. When you remove from the oven, pour off any grease and then use the aluminum foil tabs to pull the meat loaf up and out of the pan and transfer to a baking sheet. Then add the remaining sticky sauce and place under the broiler. This makes serving easy and gives the outer edges of the meat loaf a bit of crispiness.*

*Another Idea:* *Make muffin tin meat loaves by pressing the meat mixture into a standard muffin tin and baking for 20 to 30 minutes.*

PER SERVING: CALORIES: 360; TOTAL FAT: 15G; SODIUM: 934MG; CHOLESTEROL: 173MG; TOTAL CARBS: 24G; FIBER: 1G; SUGAR: 8G; PROTEIN: 33G

# Priazzo

**SERVES** 6

**PREP TIME:** 10 minutes / **COOK TIME:** 35 minutes

This recipe is pizza meets pie. My friend Briana shared it with me, and it quickly became my son's favorite meal. It's fun to assemble with pizza fillings all tucked inside a flaky pie crust.

**TOOLS AND EQUIPMENT**

deep-dish pie pan

medium skillet

stirring spoon

rubber spatula

fork

oven mitts

**INGREDIENTS**

Nonstick cooking spray, for greasing

2 refrigerated pie crusts

1 pound Italian sausage

2 (14-ounce) jars pizza sauce, divided

4 cups shredded mozzarella cheese, divided

1 (6-ounce) bag pepperoni slices

1. **Prepare the pan:** Preheat the oven to 375°F. Coat the interior of a deep-dish pie pan with nonstick spray. Unroll 1 pie crust onto the pie pan. Using your fingers, press the dough into edges so it fits snugly. Make sure it comes all the way up the sides of the pan.

2. **Brown the sausage:** Put the sausage in a medium skillet, and cook over medium heat for about 5 minutes or until browned. Remove from the heat. Drain the sausage and safely discard the grease. Spread the sausage in an even layer along the bottom of the pie pan.

3. **Layer:** Pour ½ jar of pizza sauce over the sausage, and cover with 2 cups of mozzarella. Pour another ½ jar of pizza sauce over the cheese. Add a layer of pepperoni. Pour ½ jar of pizza sauce on top, and cover with the remaining 2 cups of mozzarella. Pour the remaining ½ jar of pizza sauce over the cheese.

4. **Add the second pie crust:** Unroll the second pie crust on top. Using a fork, tuck the edges in all the way around, then prick holes for ventilation.

5. **Bake:** Place the pie pan on a baking sheet on the middle rack of the oven. Bake for 35 minutes, or until the crust is a golden brown and the pie has cooked through. Remove from the oven.

*Pro Tip:* To keep the edges of the crust from becoming overdone, cover the edges of the pie crust with foil for most of the cooking time and then remove it during the last 10 to 15 minutes of baking to brown.

*Jazz It Up:* Try these variations:

- **Roma:** Use green bell pepper, black olives, mushrooms, pepperoni, Italian sausage, ground beef, mozzarella, onion, and Cheddar.
- **Godfather:** Add Monterey Jack, Parmesan, and ricotta to the Roma variation.
- **Milano:** Pile on the Canadian bacon, but leave out the onion.
- **Florentine:** Combine five kinds of cheese: ricotta, Parmesan, Romano, mozzarella, and Cheddar. Add ham and a bit of spinach.
- **Napoli:** Add sliced tomatoes to the top layer.

PER SERVING: CALORIES: 1019; TOTAL FAT: 75G; SODIUM: 2321MG; CHOLESTEROL: 146MG; TOTAL CARBS: 46G; FIBER: 3G; SUGAR: 5G; PROTEIN: 40G

# Kielbasa and Apple Pasta Bake

NUT-FREE

**SERVES** 6

**PREP TIME:** 10 minutes / **COOK TIME:** 40 minutes

The Granny Smith apples in this Kielbasa and Apple Pasta Bake offer a sweet tartness and pop of color to this dish. The apples pair well with the kielbasa's flavor.

## TOOLS AND EQUIPMENT

2 medium saucepans

colander

whisk

9-by-13-inch baking pan

oven mitts

## INGREDIENTS

1 cup milk

2 tablespoons all-purpose flour

⅓ cup shredded Cheddar cheese

¼ teaspoon salt

⅛ teaspoon freshly ground pepper

4 ounces dry penne pasta, cooked according to the package directions

2 medium Granny Smith apples, cored and diced

4 ounces turkey kielbasa, diced

1. **Make the sauce:** Preheat the oven to 350°F. In a medium saucepan, whisk together the milk and flour. Cook, stirring, over medium heat, for about 5 minutes, or until thickened and bubbly. Remove from the heat. Add the cheese, salt, and pepper, stirring until smooth.

2. **Bake:** In a 9-by-13-inch baking pan, combine the pasta, apples, kielbasa, and sauce. Cover with aluminum foil. Place the baking pan on the middle rack of the oven, and bake for 20 minutes. Remove the foil, and bake for 15 minutes, or until the sauce bubbles around the edges. Remove from the oven.

*Pro Tip:* Combine the pasta, apples, kielbasa, and sauce in a medium mixing bowl, and toss before adding to the baking pan for better flavor integration.

PER SERVING: CALORIES: 221; TOTAL FAT: 9G; SODIUM: 332MG; CHOLESTEROL: 21MG; TOTAL CARBS: 28G; FIBER: 4G; SUGAR: 10G; PROTEIN: 8G

# Easiest Cheesiest Tortellini Bake

NUT-FREE

**SERVES** 4

**PREP TIME:** 10 minutes / **COOK TIME:** 25 minutes

If you love cheese, this recipe is for you. It's a great pasta dish that is big on flavor and easy to make. It's cheese tortellini resting in a cheesy sauce, with a pop of color from the baby spinach.

**TOOLS AND EQUIPMENT**

medium ovenproof pot

colander

stirring spoon

oven mitts

**INGREDIENTS**

1½ cups chicken broth

8 ounces cream cheese

1 teaspoon garlic powder

½ teaspoon freshly ground pepper

6 cups fresh baby spinach

1¼ pounds cheese tortellini, cooked according to the package directions

2 cups grated Colby-Jack cheese

½ cup shredded Cheddar cheese

1. **Prepare the sauce:** Preheat the oven to 400°F. In a medium ovenproof pot, combine the chicken broth, cream cheese, garlic powder, and pepper. Simmer, stirring, over medium heat for about 10 minutes, or until the cream cheese has melted and the mixture is smooth. Stir in the spinach. Cook for 5 minutes, or until the spinach has wilted. Gently stir in the tortellini. Stir in the Colby-Jack cheese. Sprinkle the Cheddar cheese on top.

2. **Bake:** Transfer the pot to the oven, and bake for 7 minutes, or until the sauce has thickened. Remove from the oven. Let rest for 5 minutes, then serve.

*Jazz It Up:* Try adding ¼ cup bread crumbs on top of the dish before putting it in the oven.

*Pro Tip:* Cut the cream cheese into 1-inch cubes before adding to the chicken broth. It will melt faster and smoother.

PER SERVING: CALORIES: 964; TOTAL FAT: 49G; SODIUM: 1854MG; CHOLESTEROL: 184MG; TOTAL CARBS: 90G; FIBER: 5G; SUGAR: 5G; PROTEIN: 42G

BROWNIES, PAGE 144

# Chapter 8

# DESSERTS

All good things come to an end—after dessert, of course. This delicious chapter shares recipes for an Easy Peach Cobbler (page 138); No Eggs, No Butter Chocolate Cake (page 141); and cookies. There's a festive fudge recipe (page 143), and my favorite might be the Peanut Butter and Chocolate Chip Cookies (page 146)—they're like the best of both worlds.

# Lemon Ice

**MAKES** 1 quart

**PREP TIME:** 5 minutes, plus 8 hours to chill / **COOK TIME:** 10 minutes

Move over, ice cream. This dessert is a lemon lover's dream. While it is easy to make, it does require several hours of freezing time. It's a great dessert to start making early in the day to serve at dinner or to make in the evening for a refreshing afternoon treat the next day.

## TOOLS AND EQUIPMENT

small mixing bowl

medium saucepan

large mixing bowl

plastic container

large spoon

## INGREDIENTS

4 lemons

1 orange

1½ cups sugar

1. **Prepare the citrus:** Cut the lemons and the orange in half. Remove the seeds. Over a small mixing bowl, squeeze until no more juice comes out of them.

2. **Make simple syrup:** In a medium saucepan, combine the water and sugar. Bring to a boil over medium-high heat and cook for 10 minutes, or until the sugar has completely dissolved and a thin syrup has formed. Remove from the heat. Pour into a large mixing bowl, and let cool.

3. **Make the ice:** Pour the simple syrup into a plastic container. Add the lemon and orange juice. Stir. Cover with plastic wrap, and freeze for 8 hours, or until hard.

4. **Serve:** Use a large spoon to scrape the mixture into shavings and shape into scoop-size servings.

*Pro Tip: Strain the juices to remove any pulp before adding to the simple syrup.*

PER SERVING (½ CUP): CALORIES: 151; TOTAL FAT: 0G; SODIUM: 5MG; CHOLESTEROL: 0MG; TOTAL CARBS: 39G; FIBER: 0G; SUGAR: 39G; PROTEIN: 0G

# Easy Fruit Tarts

**MAKES** 12 tarts
**PREP TIME:** 15 minutes / **COOK TIME:** 15 minutes

This recipe uses bread as the tart shell. These fruit tarts are one of my favorite desserts to make because I love the transformation of the bread into a crust. Filled with fruit and topped with whipped cream, these tarts present well and taste delicious.

## TOOLS AND EQUIPMENT

can opener

rolling pin

pizza cutter

pastry brush

12-cup muffin pan

oven mitts

spoon

## INGREDIENTS

12 slices bread

2 tablespoons butter, melted

1 (21-ounce) can fruit pie filling

1 (6.5-ounce) can aerosol whipped cream

1. **Make the shell:** Preheat the oven to 350°F. Using a rolling pin, press each slice of bread flat. Using a pizza cutter or knife, trim the crust off the bread slices, and make them into squares. Using a pastry brush, brush the butter onto each square. On each square, using a pizza cutter, halfway down the left edge, make a 1-inch horizontal cut, from the edge toward the center. Repeat on the right side. (Do *not* cut the bread squares in half; there should be about an inch of intact bread between the left and right cuts.) Place each square into a muffin cup. Gently overlap the "tabs" made by the left and right cuts, and press each square into the shape of the muffin cup. Transfer the muffin pan to the oven, and bake for 12 minutes, or until the bread is crisp and golden. Remove from the oven. Let cool completely in the pan.

2. **Make the tarts:** Remove the bread cups from the muffin pan, and spoon in the fruit filling. Top with whipped cream.

*Pro Tip: Cover the muffin pan with aluminum foil during the last 5 minutes of baking to prevent the tips from burning.*

PER SERVING (1 TART): CALORIES: 180; TOTAL FAT: 6G; SODIUM: 156MG; CHOLESTEROL: 20MG; TOTAL CARBS: 25G; FIBER: 2G; SUGAR: 3G; PROTEIN: 5G

# Easy Peach Cobbler

**SERVES** 16

**PREP TIME:** 10 minutes / **COOK TIME:** 1 hour

This Easy Peach Cobbler recipe is delicious and takes me back to my grandma's cooking. It's easy to make and big on taste. There are so many serving possibilities: Serve it warm with homemade whipped cream or with vanilla ice cream. Try drizzling it with homemade caramel sauce. You can even combine all three for a sensational dessert.

**TOOLS AND EQUIPMENT**

can opener

colander

3 medium mixing bowls

9-by-13-inch baking pan

stirring spoon

oven mitts

**INGREDIENTS**

2 (15-ounce) cans sliced peaches in syrup

8 tablespoons (1 stick) butter

1 cup self-rising flour (see Helpful Hint)

1 cup sugar

1 cup milk

1. **Get ready:** Preheat the oven to 350°F. Reserving the syrup, strain 1 can of peaches in a colander set over a medium mixing bowl, and put the peaches in a separate medium mixing bowl. Drain the second can of peaches (you can discard the syrup from this can). Put the butter in a 9-by-13-inch baking pan. Transfer to the oven, and heat until melted. Remove from the oven.

2. **Make the batter:** In another medium mixing bowl, mix together the flour and sugar. Mix in the milk and the reserved syrup from the peaches. Stir until smooth.

3. **Bake:** Pour the batter over the melted butter in the baking pan. Arrange the peaches over the batter in rows. Return the baking pan to the oven, and bake for 1 hour, or until the batter rises around the peaches and the crust is thick and golden brown. Remove from the oven.

*Helpful Hint: If you don't have self-rising flour, substitute 1 cup all-purpose flour mixed with 1½ teaspoons baking powder and ⅛ teaspoon salt.*

PER SERVING: CALORIES: 168; TOTAL FAT: 6G; SODIUM: 48MG; CHOLESTEROL: 17MG; TOTAL CARBS: 27G; FIBER: 1G; SUGAR: 20G; PROTEIN: 2G

# Scotch Shortbread

**MAKES** 2 dozen

**PREP TIME:** 10 minutes / **COOK TIME:** 20 minutes

We owe the origin of this recipe to a Scotswoman by the name of Mrs. McLintock. While this may not be her recipe, she is credited with having the first printed shortbread recipe, back in 1736. Shortbread is an unleavened cookie. It is best made with pure butter for that melt-in-your-mouth taste and buttery flavor.

## TOOLS AND EQUIPMENT

large mixing bowl

rolling pin

knife

baking sheet

fork

oven mitts

wire cooling rack

## INGREDIENTS

¾ cup butter

¼ cup sugar

2 cups all-purpose flour, plus more for dusting

1 to 2 tablespoons butter, softened, as needed

1. **Prepare the dough:** Preheat the oven to 350°F. In a large mixing bowl, thoroughly combine the butter and sugar. Work in the flour with your clean hands (if the dough is crumbly, mix in 1 to 2 tablespoons softened butter).

2. **Make the cookies:** Lightly flour a work surface. Turn out the dough onto the work surface, and roll out to ½- to ⅓-inch thickness. Using a knife, cut into small squares, or use small cookie cutters to create small shapes.

3. **Bake:** Place the cookies ½ inch apart on a baking sheet. Using a fork, pierce the cookies. Transfer the baking sheet to the oven, and bake for about 20 minutes or until set. Remove from the oven. Immediately transfer to a wire cooling rack, and let cool.

*Pro Tip: Try chilling the dough in the refrigerator for 30 minutes before rolling out. This will firm up the dough and help keep the cookies from spreading when baking.*

PER SERVING (1 COOKIE): CALORIES: 105; TOTAL FAT: 7G; SODIUM: 48MG; CHOLESTEROL: 18MG; TOTAL CARBS: 10G; FIBER: 0G; SUGAR: 2G; PROTEIN: 1G

# 3-Ingredient Peanut Butter Cookies

**MAKES** 14 cookies
**PREP TIME:** 5 minutes / **COOK TIME:** 10 minutes

When my friend Briana was in seventh grade, she took home economics. These 3-Ingredient Peanut Butter Cookies were the first cookies she made. She taught her grandfather to make these, then her son, and me. They remain a family favorite at her house, and we find them so easy, they are one of ours, too.

**TOOLS AND EQUIPMENT**

medium mixing bowl

stirring spoon

teaspoon

baking sheet

fork

oven mitts

**INGREDIENTS**

2 cups sugar

1 cup peanut butter

1 large egg

1. **Make the dough:** Preheat the oven to 350°F. In a medium mixing bowl, combine the sugar, peanut butter, and egg. Mix until well incorporated.

2. **Shape the cookies:** Scoop the dough by the teaspoon onto a baking sheet. Use a fork to press in one direction, then in the other direction to make a "tic-tac-toe" looking grid.

3. **Bake:** Transfer the baking sheet to the oven, and bake for 10 minutes, or until golden. Remove from the oven.

*Pro Tip: Creamy peanut butter will work the best. Roll the teaspoon-size dough into a ball before placing on the baking sheet for a more uniformly shaped batch.*

PER SERVING (1 COOKIE): CALORIES: 221; TOTAL FAT: 10G; SODIUM: 90MG; CHOLESTEROL: 13MG; TOTAL CARBS: 32G; FIBER: 1G; SUGAR: 30G; PROTEIN: 5G

# No Eggs, No Butter Chocolate Cake

DAIRY-FREE, NUT-FREE, VEGAN

**MAKES** 1 (8-by-8-inch) cake
**PREP TIME:** 5 minutes / **COOK TIME:** 35 minutes

This recipe is unusual because it has no butter and no eggs and still creates a moist, fluffy cake. The best part is that you mix it right in the pan, so there are no extra bowls to clean.

## TOOLS AND EQUIPMENT

8-by-8-inch baking pan

spoon

oven mitts

## INGREDIENTS

5 tablespoons vegetable oil, plus more for greasing

1½ cups all-purpose flour

1 cup sugar

3 tablespoons unsweetened cocoa

1 teaspoon baking soda

½ teaspoon salt

1 teaspoon white vinegar

1 teaspoon pure vanilla extract

1 cup water

Frosting, for topping

1. **Prepare the cake:** Preheat the oven to 350°F. Grease an 8-by-8-inch baking pan. Add the flour, sugar, cocoa, baking soda, and salt. Mix well. Make 1 large well and 2 small wells. Pour the vinegar into one of the small wells and vanilla in the other. Pour the oil into the large well. Pour the water into the pan, and mix well until smooth.

2. **Bake:** Place the baking pan on the middle rack of the oven for 35 minutes, or until a toothpick inserted into the center comes out clean. Remove from the oven. Let cool completely, then top with your favorite frosting.

*Pro Tip:* Put a tub of store-bought chocolate frosting in the microwave for 30 seconds, stir it, and pour it on top of the cake for a perfectly smooth frosting.

*Another Idea:* You can double the recipe and use a 9-by-13-inch baking pan. Check the cake after 35 minutes, and if it is not done, add another 5 minutes.

PER SERVING (1/16): CALORIES: 131; TOTAL FAT: 5G; SODIUM: 153MG; CHOLESTEROL: 0MG; TOTAL CARBS: 22G; FIBER: 1G; SUGAR: 13G; PROTEIN: 1G

# Banana Cream Pie

**MAKES** 1 (9-inch) pie
**PREP TIME:** 10 minutes, plus 3 hours to chill

My grandmother Charlotte the Great used to bake pies all the time. You would walk into her kitchen and see pies everywhere, and her 4-foot-8-inch self pouring more filling into a pie shell. One of her favorite pies to make was Banana Cream Pie, which was my grandfather's favorite pie. This is her recipe. I remember she was embarrassed when I asked her for it because, as she said, "It's so easy!"

**TOOLS AND EQUIPMENT**

medium mixing bowl

whisk

**INGREDIENTS**

1 (5.1-ounce) box instant banana pudding

1½ cups milk

1 cup whipped topping, plus more for serving

2 or 3 medium bananas, cut into ¼-inch slices, plus more for serving

1 (6-ounce) premade graham cracker pie crust

1. **Make the filling:** In a medium mixing bowl, whisk together the pudding and milk for 2 to 3 minutes, or until it starts to thicken. Fold in the whipped topping. Lay the banana slices on the bottom of the graham cracker crust. If you have any leftover banana slices, quarter them, and add to the pudding mixture. Pour the filling into the pie crust over the banana slices.

2. **Set the pie:** Refrigerate the pie for at least 3 hours. Before serving, top with whipped topping and fresh bananas.

*Jazz It Up: Garnish with vanilla-flavored wafer cookies.*

*Store It: Keep the pie loosely covered with aluminum foil in the refrigerator for up to 3 days.*

PER SERVING: CALORIES: 227; TOTAL FAT: 7G; SODIUM: 364MG; CHOLESTEROL: 8MG; TOTAL CARBS: 39G; FIBER: 2G; SUGAR: 24G; PROTEIN: 3G

# Chocolate Fudge

**MAKES** 48 pieces

**PREP TIME:** 10 minutes, plus 2 hours to cool / **COOK TIME:** 10 minutes

I have fond memories of my mom making batches of fudge during the holidays. She'd cut it into squares and send it off to family and friends. As an adult, I tried making it, and although it was good, it required a lot of stirring and then quick action. It turns out there is an easier way. This recipe is one of the easiest fudge recipes I have ever made, and it creates delicious chocolate fudge.

## TOOLS AND EQUIPMENT

can opener

8-by-8-inch baking pan

large saucepan

stirring spoon

rubber spatula

## INGREDIENTS

Nonstick cooking spray, for greasing

24 ounces chocolate chips

2 (14-ounce) cans sweetened condensed milk

¾ teaspoon salt

2 teaspoons pure vanilla extract

1. **Melt the chocolate:** Line an 8-by-8-inch baking pan with aluminum foil and coat with nonstick cooking spray. In a large saucepan, combine the chocolate chips, condensed milk, and salt. Cook, stirring continuously, over low heat for about 6 minutes, or until the chocolate has melted and becomes thick and shiny (see Pro Tip). Remove from the heat. Stir in the vanilla.

2. **Set the fudge:** Pour the fudge into the baking pan. Using a rubber spatula, spread the fudge out to the edge and into an even layer. Let cool at room temperature for 2 hours before slicing.

*Pro Tip:* The time on the chocolate is an estimate. You are going to keep stirring until the chocolate becomes glossy. As soon as it does, remove from the heat.

PER SERVING: CALORIES: 125; TOTAL FAT: 6G; SODIUM: 56MG; CHOLESTEROL: 6MG; TOTAL CARBS: 18G; FIBER: 1G; SUGAR: 17G; PROTEIN: 1G

# Brownies

**MAKES** 1 (9-by-13-inch) pan
**PREP TIME:** 5 minutes / **COOK TIME:** 25 minutes

This brownie recipe was a favorite growing up. I've tried brownie mixes, but I think this recipe is just as easy, and it creates moist, delicious, chocolaty brownies that my family loves. They are so easy to make, they might become your signature dessert.

## TOOLS AND EQUIPMENT

9-by-13-inch baking pan

medium mixing bowl

whisk

wooden spoon

oven mitts

## INGREDIENTS

1 cup shortening, plus more for greasing

2 cups sugar

4 large eggs

¼ cup plus 3 tablespoons cocoa powder

1½ cups flour

½ teaspoon baking powder

½ teaspoon salt

1 cup walnuts (optional)

Powdered sugar, for topping (optional)

1. **Make the batter:** Preheat the oven to 350°F. Grease a 9-by-13-inch baking pan. In a medium mixing bowl, beat the shortening and sugar until creamy and fluffy. Add the eggs, one at a time, and beat well after each addition. Stir in the cocoa. Slowly add the flour, baking powder, salt, and walnuts (if using). Pour into the baking pan.

2. **Bake:** Place the baking pan on the middle rack of the oven. Bake for 25 minutes, or until a toothpick inserted into the center comes out clean. Lightly dust with powdered sugar (if desired).

*Pro Tip: Do not overstir the batter. Just stir enough to incorporate the dry ingredients.*

PER SERVING (1/18 PAN): CALORIES: 243; TOTAL FAT: 13G; SODIUM: 82MG; CHOLESTEROL: 41MG; TOTAL CARBS: 32G; FIBER: 1G; SUGAR: 22G; PROTEIN: 3G

# Microwave Chocolate Mug Cake

**SERVES** 1

**PREP TIME:** 5 minutes / **COOK TIME:** 1 minute 10 seconds

If you're cooking for one, you may still want dessert, and this chocolate mug cake is the perfect solution. It's rich and moist, just like chocolate cake should be. Better yet, it takes just a few minutes to make.

## TOOLS AND EQUIPMENT

medium mixing bowl

stirring spoon

large microwave-safe mug

microwave-safe plate

## INGREDIENTS

¼ cup all-purpose flour

2 tablespoons unsweetened cocoa powder

2 tablespoons granulated sugar

¼ teaspoon baking powder

⅛ teaspoon salt

2 tablespoons vegetable oil

¼ cup milk

1. **Combine the dry ingredients:** In a medium mixing bowl, combine the flour, cocoa, sugar, baking powder, and salt. Mix well.

2. **Make the cake:** Add the oil to the dry ingredients, and stir. Add the milk, and stir until smooth. Pour into a large microwave-safe mug. Place the mug on a microwave-safe plate or paper towel. Microwave on high for 1 minute 10 seconds, or until the cake rises.

*Pro Tip:* Keep in mind that all microwaves vary, and you may need to adjust the time. Keep an eye on it as it cooks.

*Another Tip:* You may need an additional tablespoon of milk if your batter is too thick.

*Jazz It Up:* Add a tablespoon of chocolate chips to the batter for a double chocolate surprise.

PER SERVING: CALORIES: 508; TOTAL FAT: 31G; SODIUM: 323MG; CHOLESTEROL: 5MG; TOTAL CARBS: 57G; FIBER: 5G; SUGAR: 27G; PROTEIN: 7G

# Peanut Butter and Chocolate Chip Cookies

EXTRA QUICK, VEGETARIAN

**MAKES** 36 cookies
**PREP TIME:** 15 minutes / **COOK TIME:** 15 minutes

These Peanut Butter and Chocolate Chip Cookies are my guilty pleasure. I love them warm, right out of the oven. The texture resembles chocolate chip cookies more than peanut butter cookies; these cookies are the best of both worlds.

## TOOLS AND EQUIPMENT

baking sheet

large mixing bowl

electric mixer

rubber spatula

tablespoon

oven mitts

wire cooling rack

## INGREDIENTS

1 cup (2 sticks) butter, at room temperature

1 cup creamy peanut butter

1 cup sugar

1 cup packed brown sugar

2 large eggs

½ teaspoon pure vanilla extract

2 cups all-purpose flour

1 teaspoon baking soda

2 cups semisweet chocolate chips

1. **Prepare the dough:** Preheat the oven to 325°F. Line a baking sheet with parchment paper (this is the secret to beautiful cookies). In a large mixing bowl, using an electric mixer on medium-high speed, cream the butter until smooth. Add the peanut butter, sugar, and brown sugar. Beat until fluffy. Add the eggs one at a time, beating well after each addition. Add the vanilla. Gradually stir in the flour. Add the baking soda, and mix until well combined. Using a rubber spatula, fold in the chocolate chips.

2. **Bake:** Scoop the dough by the tablespoon onto the prepared baking sheet, leaving 2 inches between cookies. Transfer the baking sheet to the oven, and bake for 15 minutes, or until firm just around the edges. They may not look done, but it's okay, remove them from the oven anyway. Slide the parchment paper with the cookies carefully off the baking sheet and onto a wire cooling rack.

*Pro Tip: If you are making more than one dozen cookies, have a second cookie sheet lined up for easy rotation. Also, you can shake the crumbs off the parchment paper and reuse it.*

*Store It:* Keep the cookies in an airtight container. I bake one dozen cookies at a time. I roll the rest of the dough into balls, and place them in a gallon-size resealable bag and freeze. I can then remove a dozen cookie balls and serve warm cookies on a whim.

PER SERVING (1 COOKIE): CALORIES: 215; TOTAL FAT: 13G; SODIUM: 110MG; CHOLESTEROL: 24MG; TOTAL CARBS: 24G; FIBER: 1G; SUGAR: 16G; PROTEIN: 3G

# MEASUREMENTS AND CONVERSIONS

## Volume Equivalents (Liquid)

| US STANDARD | US STANDARD (OUNCES) | METRIC (APPROXIMATE) |
|---|---|---|
| 2 tablespoons | 1 fl. oz. | 30 mL |
| ¼ cup | 2 fl. oz. | 60 mL |
| ½ cup | 4 fl. oz. | 120 mL |
| 1 cup | 8 fl. oz. | 240 mL |
| 1½ cups | 12 fl. oz. | 355 mL |
| 2 cups or 1 pint | 16 fl. oz. | 475 mL |
| 4 cups or 1 quart | 32 fl. oz. | 1 L |
| 1 gallon | 128 fl. oz. | 4 L |

## Oven Temperatures

| FAHRENHEIT (F) | CELSIUS (C) (APPROXIMATE) |
|---|---|
| 250° | 120° |
| 300° | 150° |
| 325° | 165° |
| 350° | 180° |
| 375° | 190° |
| 400° | 200° |
| 425° | 220° |
| 450° | 230° |

## Volume Equivalents (Dry)

| US STANDARD | METRIC (APPROXIMATE) |
|---|---|
| ⅛ teaspoon | 0.5 mL |
| ¼ teaspoon | 1 mL |
| ½ teaspoon | 2 mL |
| ¾ teaspoon | 4 mL |
| 1 teaspoon | 5 mL |
| 1 tablespoon | 15 mL |
| ¼ cup | 59 mL |
| ⅓ cup | 79 mL |
| ½ cup | 118 mL |
| ⅔ cup | 156 mL |
| ¾ cup | 177 mL |
| 1 cup | 235 mL |
| 2 cups or 1 pint | 475 mL |
| 3 cups | 700 mL |
| 4 cups or 1 quart | 1 L |

## Weight Equivalents

| US STANDARD | METRIC (APPROXIMATE) |
|---|---|
| ½ ounce | 15 g |
| 1 ounce | 30 g |
| 2 ounces | 60 g |
| 4 ounces | 115 g |
| 8 ounces | 225 g |
| 12 ounces | 340 g |
| 16 ounces or 1 pound | 455 g |

# INDEX

# ABOUT THE AUTHOR

 **Julee Morrison** is a blogger and mother of six who lives in the foothills of Virginia with two dogs. Her first book, *The Instant Pot® College Cookbook: 75 Quick and Easy Meals that Taste Like Home,* celebrates her family recipes and making quick meals everyone will love.

CPSIA information can be obtained
at www.ICGtesting.com
Printed in the USA
BVHW060539260121
598603BV00003B/3